Faith
CAN MOVE MOUNTAINS

God, Help My Unbelief

Dear Sally,
May God bless you and lead you.
Tina Pitamber

DR. TINA PITAMBER

FAITH CAN MOVE MOUNTAINS
Copyright © 2025 by Dr. Tina Pitamber

All rights reserved. Neither this publication nor any part of this publication may be reproduced or transmitted in any form or by any means, electronic or mechanical, including photocopying, recording or any information storage and retrieval system, without permission in writing from the author.

Unless otherwise indicated, Scripture quotations re taken from the Holy Bible, NEW INTERNATIONAL VERSION®, NIV® Copyright © 1973, 1978, 1984, 2011 by Biblica, Inc.® Used by permission. All rights reserved worldwide. • Scripture quotations marked (NKJV) are taken from the New King James Version®. Copyright © 1982 by Thomas Nelson. Used by permission. All rights reserved.

Printed in Canada

ISBN: 978-1-4866-2715-8
eBook ISBN: 978-1-4866-2716-5

Word Alive Press
119 De Baets Street Winnipeg, MB R2J 3R9
www.wordalivepress.ca

WORD ALIVE
—PRESS—

MIX
Paper | Supporting responsible forestry
FSC® C103567

Cataloguing in Publication information can be obtained from Library and Archives Canada.

Dedication

TO MY SISTERS—Pramila, Tania, Lisa, and Selena. God has blessed us with sisterhood. I love you and am grateful for your love and support.

DEDICATION	iii
INTRODUCTION	vii
1: FAITH STARTS WITH BELIEVING IN GOD	1
2: FAITH AND FORGIVENESS OF SIN	6
3: FAITH AND GOD'S HEALING	13
4: FAITH AND GOD'S PROVISION	26
5: FAITH AND ACTION	46
6: FAITH AND BOLDNESS	56
7: CORPORATE FAITH	65
8: PERSEVERING FAITH	73
9: WAVERING FAITH	84
10: FAITH AND WAITING	93
11: MODELLING FAITH	101
12: FAITH AND OBEDIENCE	108
13: FAITH AND TESTING	116
14: FAITH AND WITNESS	122
15: GOD IS FAITHFUL	127

Introduction

HAVE YOU EVER poured out your heart to someone about a desperate situation in your life, and their response was simply, "Trust God and have faith"? Even though you knew that the person had good intentions, something about that response irked you. Rather than feeling comforted, you felt frustrated, because what you were going through wasn't just any situation. It was a serious situation, like your mother dying, or the doctor telling you to prepare for a surgery, or your spouse asking for a divorce. The last thing you wanted to hear from someone was "Trust God and have faith," because you weren't sure how you were going to get through your situation and if you were going to make it.

At times I have said those very same words—"Trust God and have faith"—to others when they've shared deep and difficult things about their life with me. But when those same words were echoed to me, I felt that the response was a cop-out, because my need was great, and the answer was too spiritual. However, despite how I was feeling about my situation, this answer was exactly what I needed to hear and do. I simply needed to have faith—specifically, faith in God.

Of course, instead of trusting God, at times I've been guilty of putting my faith in things or people. You might be thinking, *No, that can't be true.* Well, it's true for all of us. Whether we realize it or not, we exercise faith in different things or people, rather than God. For example, if you're married, perhaps you put your faith in your spouse, because you depend on him/her to feel loved. If you're a parent, maybe you look to your children to bring joy to your life. If you have money, investments, a home, and a car, perhaps you trust those things to make you feel secure.

But what does the Bible say about faith and where we should place it? If you survey the Scriptures, you will find that faith is a significant topic. One book of the Bible in particular, Hebrews, contains an entire section dedicated to defining faith and identifying people who practised faith: *"Now faith is confidence in what we hope for and assurance about what we do not see"* (Hebrews 11:1). But what does that mean? One commentary describes faith like this:

> The beginning point of faith is believing in God's character—he is who he says. The end point is believing in God's promises—he will do what he says. When we believe that God will fulfill his promises even though we don't see those promises materializing yet, we demonstrate faith.[1]

Still scratching your head? Let me break it down for you. According to the Bible, faith is first believing in God and His character. This means you believe that there is a God who exists, and you trust and have full confidence in Him. Second, faith means you believe God will do what He says (promises). This means you believe in His Word even though you can't see how it will come to pass. That's faith. Let that definition of faith sink in, because maybe you haven't heard it like this before, yet this is what faith is.

---

[1] *Life Application Study Bible—New International Version* (Carol Stream, IL: Tyndale House Publishers, 1997), 2236.

Now that you know what faith is, you might be wondering how it impacts your life. In one word—tremendously. Faith in God and His promises can produce profound experiences and blessings in our lives. By faith, God can heal us from sickness, provide for our financial needs, free us from the bondage of sin, and give us eternal life in heaven after death. This is all possible because of faith!

Sadly, few people get to see the hand of God move in their lives, or experience the promises of God manifested in their lives because they simply lack faith in God. I'm not saying faith is like some magic potion to make all our dreams and wishes come true. God is not Santa Claus, where we tell Him what we want and He's obligated to make it happen. God will do what He does according to His purpose and plan. But when faith is present, amazing things can happen!

So where do you stand? Do you have faith in God, or do you have some uncertainty in your heart? If you're not sure about life and God, maybe you have unbelief. We might think that traces of doubt in our hearts about God and His plan are no big deal, but it is a big deal. Because when faith is lacking, other things creep into our lives that can impact us in a negative way—things like fear, anxiety, depression, despair, anger, frustration, and bitterness. This is not what God wants for us; rather, He calls us to have faith in Him so that we can experience His peace, mercy, love, and goodness. But we can only have access to those things by faith in God.

That's what this book is all about. It's about faith in God and His promises, and asking God to remove any unbelief. I believe that God wants to increase our faith in Him, and I hope that after reading this book, your eyes will be opened to see all the wonderful things that can happen when you choose to have faith. If you're ready, let's begin this journey!

One

FAITH STARTS WITH BELIEVING IN GOD

THE STARTING POINT of faith is believing in God's character, but to believe in His character, we need to believe first that there is a God.

When I was a child, I'd get up in the morning, go to school, come home, complete my homework, watch television shows, do some chores, and go to bed. The next day, I'd do the same thing, and the day after that would be the same. Do you know what I did the day after that? You guessed it—the same thing. It was like life was on autopilot or repeat. It was routine. Even though I was young, I understood that there had to be more to life than what I was doing daily. For me, life was bigger than routine. No, scratch that—someone bigger had to be out there.

As a young child, I would observe the places and people around me. Sometimes when I walked to school or was in the grocery store, I could tell if people were happy, sad, or angry. When I was around people, I could sense if something wasn't right. It was as though there was an invisible heaviness that hung over people. I couldn't pinpoint what it was about at the time, but now that I'm older, I understand that the people weren't right because they were disconnected from God.

That was true for my life. I was also disconnected from God, but that changed for me when a woman from the Church of the Nazarene in our area bravely knocked on our door and invited my mother to church. Her courage led my mother to take all four of us children—my sisters and me—to church. At that time, I was only eight years old.

During the second worship service we attended, they dismissed the children to attend the Sunday school class. We all went downstairs for our time of learning, and on that Sunday, we watched a movie depicting the life of Jesus. In the movie, I saw Jesus teaching and helping people. I saw the good moments in His life, but the movie also showed the hard things Jesus walked through.

I can't explain all the emotions I felt as I watched this innocent man, who'd done nothing wrong to anyone, being abused, flogged, beaten, and then told to carry a cross. Then I saw Him being crucified, and blood ran down His body as He hung on the cross. I thought, *Why are they treating Jesus like this? He's an innocent man; He didn't do anything wrong.* My heart sank as I continued to watch the movie. I thought, *This is how His life is going to end. He's going to die.* My mind was racing, and I wondered why they were showing that movie to us. It was so sad and discouraging. I didn't understand.

But just when I thought it was over for Jesus, a bright light shone in the movie as they showed His tomb. Then I saw that the grave was empty, and Jesus appeared on the movie screen—healthy and alive! All of a sudden, my feelings of sadness turned into joy. Whatever they did to Him, it didn't stop Him. Somehow Jesus escaped death!

The dark room I was in was now filled with light. As my Sunday school teacher turned off the movie and turned on the lights, my head was spinning with questions. I had mixed emotions about the movie. The teacher explained the significance of Jesus's suffering, death, and resurrection. She told us that Jesus was God and had died for our sins, and if we wanted our sins to be forgiven, we could receive Christ, and we would be saved. Then she asked the question, "Does anyone want to give their hearts to Jesus?"

Although I was only eight years old and had just learned about Jesus, something in my heart told me that I needed to receive Him. I bravely put my hand up and opened my heart to Jesus. The Sunday school teacher led us in the prayer of repentance and acceptance of Jesus. When I opened my eyes after she prayed, my heart was changed. Whatever heaviness I'd felt was no longer there. I felt like a key had been given to me, and God's love unlocked a floodgate of closed doors. I sensed a deep peace in my heart that I didn't have before. I no longer was walking in the dark. I was in the light!

To receive Jesus Christ, I needed to exercise faith. I couldn't see Jesus, but I believed that what I'd seen in the movie and what my Sunday school teacher had said was true. I believed by faith. This is the starting point—believing by faith that God exists. The writer of Hebrews says, *"By faith we understand that the universe was formed at God's command, so that what is seen was not made out of what was visible"* (Hebrews 11:3). This verse explains that God created the world, and we believe God exists by faith. Do you believe this?

At some point, you'll need to decide for yourself if you believe there's a God or not. Whatever you believe about God will affect everything else in your life. If you don't believe in God, then by default you have faith in things or people (work, children, money). Let me ask you a question: How is putting your faith in people and things working for you? Do you have a sense of purpose and fulfillment in your heart?

Perhaps you're like Nicodemus in the Bible. Nicodemus was a Pharisee who belonged to a Jewish religious group that followed the Old Testament laws as well as their traditions. He held a high status in his society. Nicodemus knew about Jesus, but he didn't believe in Jesus. He was an outsider looking in.

In John 3, Nicodemus has a conversation with Jesus and says, "*Rabbi, we know you are a teacher who has come from God. For no one could perform the miraculous signs you are doing if God were not with him*" (John 3:2b). Nicodemus acknowledges that Jesus is knowledgeable and powerful, but he hasn't taken the steps to believe that Jesus is God.

Jesus responds to Nicodemus and says something to the effect of, "I want to share more with you, but because you don't believe in the basic things that are plain to you, I can't talk to you about the things of God you cannot see" (John 3:10–14, paraphrase). A modern-day translation of this might be: "Nicodemus, if you or someone you know has been healed, has received a financial blessing, has given birth to a child, or has witnessed someone set free from addiction, and you don't believe in the miracles in front of you, then how can I talk to you about things like heaven or eternal life?"

Perhaps like Nicodemus, you've experienced miracles in your life, but you're just not sure if God exists. Or maybe the opposite is true—you've seen little of the hand of God in your life, so you simply don't believe He exists.

• • •

THE MOST IMPORTANT QUESTION YOU'LL NEED TO SETTLE FOR YOURSELF IS IF YOU BELIEVE IN GOD. ACCORDING TO THE BIBLE, THERE IS A GOD AND YOU BELIEVE THAT HE EXISTS BY FAITH.

• • •

If you're still not sure, the next chapter will be vital in your journey and will hopefully answer your questions about God, Jesus, and why we need to put our faith in Jesus Christ.

Two

FAITH AND FORGIVENESS OF SIN

PERHAPS YOU BELIEVE in God and believe that Jesus Christ is your Saviour—and if you do, you may just want to skip this chapter and move on to Chapter Three. But if you're still struggling to understand whether there is a God and why we need to believe in Him, this chapter will help you understand the extent of His love and the reasons you exist.

EVERYTHING WAS GOOD

Let's start right from the beginning. According to the Bible, the Spirit of God hovered over the waters as God created the heavens and the earth, light, the sky, land, vegetation, creatures, and livestock in the first five days (Genesis 1:1–25). On the sixth day, God created Adam and Eve, the first two humans (Genesis 1:27). After God created the world and humans, the Bible says that "*God saw all that he had made, and it was very good*" (Genesis 1:31a).

Let's pause right there. Pay attention to what God's Word says. God saw *all* that He had made and it was very *good*. If you think about it, our human storyline doesn't begin with an acknowledgement that we are "bad." It actually starts with the revelation that we're good. This marks the beginning point of our human creation story: we were good.

Because everything was good for Adam and Eve—they had a good relationship with God, with each other, and with the Garden of Eden—they walked naked and they didn't feel any shame (Genesis 2:25). Unfortunately, their lives of purity were short-lived. Their relationship with God changed once they encountered the serpent (Satan).

THE FALL

In Genesis 3, Eve is tempted by Satan. Who is Satan? According to the Bible, he's a fallen angel (Luke 10:18) created by God for good but who chose to rebel against Him. Satan is a real person and not a made-up entity. Some people don't believe there are evil forces or entities out there, but they do exist (Ephesians 6:12). I'm puzzled by how many people watch movies about good and evil yet won't believe there are real invisible good and evil forces in the spiritual realm around us.

Satan's mission is to cause people to stray from God (1 Peter 5:8), which is what he did to Eve. Satan had a conversation with Eve and asks her this question: *"Did God really say, 'You must not eat from any tree in the garden?'"* (Genesis 3:1b). Why did Satan ask this? Because he wanted her to doubt what God had already told her. Eve responds by saying that she would die if she ate from the tree of knowledge (Genesis 2:16–17). Satan replies, *"You will not certainly die"* (Genesis 3:4a), adding that if she ate the fruit, she'd be like God in terms of knowing both good and evil (Genesis 3:5).

This conversation shows how Satan twists what God says, but we can't trust him, because he's a liar (John 8:44). God had told Adam and Eve that they would die if they ate from the forbidden tree, and Satan told Eve the exact opposite. This is how the enemy works. God says one thing, but Satan tells us something else. Due to this lie, Satan ended up deceiving Eve.

Well, too bad for her, we might think. *It's her fault.*

Eve was gullible and not very smart for listening to Satan. But does the apple fall far from the tree? The answer is no. Unfortunately, we've fallen for the same trick. We forget about God's Word and listen to Satan's voice instead. God's Word tells us not to lie (Exodus 20:16), yet we lie. God's Word tells us to forgive those who have mistreated us (Luke 11:4), yet we don't forgive. The Bible tells us to honour our mother and father (Exodus 20:12), yet we dishonour our parents.

But Eve listened to what Satan said and ate from the forbidden tree. She then gave some of the fruit to her husband, Adam. As a result, their eyes were opened. Their act of disobedience made them realize that they were naked, and they felt shame and had to cover themselves with fig leaves (Genesis 3:7).

When Adam and Eve realized their sin, they tried to hide from God. Everything that had been good for this couple became tainted because of their disobedience.

Indeed, their one act of sin had many implications. First, every person born after them was born with a sinful nature (Psalm 51:5). Second, their sin caused death to enter the world (Genesis 2:16–17). Third, they became spiritually disconnected from God. This is why we have a sinful nature, why death has entered the world, and why we are alienated from God and are His enemies (Colossians 1:21). It's all because of sin!

What a tragedy it is, for Adam and Eve and for us today as well. *We're doomed*, we might think. *There's no hope for us, no hope for humanity.* But think again! The good news is that our story doesn't end there.

REDEMPTION

God didn't plan for us to fall into sin; rather, He always wanted a loving relationship with us. But Adam and Eve's sin put Him in a dilemma. I guess you can say a pickle. How was God going to save us, since every person born after them would have a sinful nature? Somehow God needed to satisfy the consequence of sin and at the same time save us from death and eternal separation from Him.

If you were God, how would you fix this? Unsure of an answer? That's because there's only *one* answer: Jesus. Why is Jesus the answer? Because He is God (John 10:30). Jesus is the exact representation of God (Hebrews 1:3). He was conceived by the Holy Spirit (Matthew 1:20) and was sinless (2 Corinthians 5:21).

Because of these truths, Jesus is the perfect solution to God's problem. Only Jesus could satisfy the consequence of our sin and save us from sin and death. Why? Because only a sinless person can save us. Think about it like this: In a conversation about sin, one of my colleagues said that you don't clean a dirty table with a dirty rag. You use a clean one. That's why Jesus is the only One who can save us, because He's pure, holy, clean, and perfect.

Without Jesus, we will sin, die, and be eternally separated from God. We naturally do what is wrong because of our sinful nature. What do I mean? The Bible says "*The acts of the flesh are obvious: sexual immorality, impurity and debauchery; idolatry and witchcraft; hatred, discord, jealousy, fits of rage, selfish ambition, dissensions, factions and envy; drunkenness, orgies, and the like*" (Galatians 5:19–21a). This is how we live before knowing Jesus—in sin. We might not think sin is a big deal, but based on the Bible, we know it carries major consequences for us. Our sin leads us to death (Romans 6:23).

Our sin is like a crime against God. In a just society when someone commits a crime, that person is tried through the justice system, and a verdict is reached based on the evidence. That person will have to comply with the verdict and the subsequent sentence. The same is true with our sinful behaviour against God. The ultimate penalty for our sin is death. Our debt is high, and we can't pay it.

You might be wondering why you had to read this chapter if the future is doom and gloom. Is there any hope for us? Yes! Our story doesn't end there. Our sin leads to death, but God's love leads to life! Instead of us paying for our sins, Jesus paid the price. Instead of us dying for our sins, Jesus took our place and hung on a cross. Instead of us making a sacrifice to God, Jesus sacrificed Himself to pay our sin penalty. Instead of us making it right with God, Jesus atoned for our sins.

> You see, at just the right time, when we were still powerless, Christ died for the ungodly. Very rarely will anyone die for a righteous person, though for a good person someone might possibly dare to die. But God demonstrates his own love for us in this: While we were still sinners, Christ died for us. (Romans 5:6–8)

Jesus Christ paid our debt and saved our lives! Therefore, we don't have to live in sin, die, or be disconnected from God. Instead, we can be free from our sins (John 8:36), live a good and pleasing life to God (Galatians 5:22–23), enjoy eternal life (John 3:16), and be connected to God (John 1:12).

If all of this is true, how do we gain freedom from sin, reconnect with God, and have eternal life? Simply by faith! Paul writes, *"For it is by grace, you have been saved, through faith—and this is not from yourselves, it is the gift of God—not by works, so that no one can boast"* (Ephesians 2:8–9).

That's it? By faith? Yes! Is it really that simple? Yes! We don't receive God's favour through our works, such as giving to the poor, helping the needy, donating money, or serving others. Rather, we're saved by God's grace (mercy, compassion, and love) through faith. We simply believe that Jesus is Lord, that He saved us from our sin through His death and resurrection, and that through Him we have forgiveness of sins and eternal life. Faith is the key to the doorway of salvation, but grace is why we are saved.

• • •

> FAITH IS THE KEY TO THE DOORWAY OF SALVATION, BUT GRACE IS WHY WE ARE SAVED.

• • •

Why would God do this for us? Because of love! Love is why God created us. It's why Jesus hung on a cross and died for us and then rose on the third day. Even though we exercised our free will and turned away from God, He didn't turn away from us; instead, Jesus satisfied the law and paid the penalty for our sins so that He could have a relationship with us. Jesus died in our place—all because of love.

Why does this matter? Because your life has a purpose. My life has a purpose. We're not random people living on earth. There is a God out there who loved us enough to die for us. Understanding this gives life new meaning. What we used to put our faith in, such as people and things, no longer matters, because now our faith in God changes how we live. We no longer desire to sin but to grow and mature in the Lord. This is the journey we're on until we die or Jesus Christ returns.

INVITATION

As my Sunday school teacher asked me, I now ask you: Do you want to put your faith and trust in Jesus Christ now that we understand that we are sinners and need a Saviour? If so, we can say by faith, "I believe Jesus is God and that He died for me." Paul writes, *"If you declare with your mouth, 'Jesus is Lord,' and believe in your heart that God raised him from the dead, you will be saved"* (Romans 10:9).

A new life in Christ is just a step of faith away. If you feel led, say this prayer below:

> Jesus, I now understand that I have sinned against God, and I need to confess my sin to you. I believe that you are God and that you died on the cross for my sins. I believe that you rose on the third day and that now my sins are forgiven. I receive you as my Lord and Saviour and want to have eternal life. In Jesus's name, amen.

If you said this prayer, by faith you have received Jesus as your Saviour. Praise the Lord! Welcome to the family of God! You are now a child of God.

Three

FAITH AND GOD'S HEALING

CAN GOD HEAL a person? Some people don't believe that healing is possible, whereas others believe that God doesn't heal due to a lack of faith. Based on my life experience, I would steer clear of both trains of thought, because they're too extreme.

Sometimes when I've prayed for people they've been healed, but other times, those I prayed for were not healed. We can't say why someone was healed and someone else wasn't, because we don't know why. But when someone is sick and faith in God is present, that person can experience divine healing. I don't say this because I'm hopeful but because the Bible records that when the people exercised faith in God, healing was possible. Let's look at who was healed in the Bible and how it took place.

HEALED BY GOD'S WORD
In Matthew 8, we read about a Roman centurion who approached Jesus. His servant was at home, sick and paralyzed. When Jesus heard about the situation, He told the centurion that He would go and heal him. But read how the Roman centurion responded to Jesus:

> ... Lord, I do not deserve to have you come under my roof. But just say the word, and my servant will be healed. For I myself am a man under authority, with soldiers under me. I tell this one, "Go," and he goes; and that one, "Come," and he comes. I say to my servant, "Do this," and he does it. (Matthew 8:8–9)

Wow! When Jesus heard the Roman centurion's response, He was amazed at his faith. Jesus said that He hadn't found anyone in Israel with faith like that (Matthew 8:10).

When we or someone we know is sick, we can have faith that God can heal, because He can do the impossible. Many times in the Bible when God's people had faith in Him, He worked in their situations. Do you have faith that God can heal you and others? You might be thinking, *I want to believe, but sometimes I doubt God in this area.* Well, my friends, God wants us to have faith.

Think about it like this. Faith is like the gas in your car's tank. Without the gas, the car is stuck. Faith is also like the battery in a flashlight. Without the battery, the flashlight can't produce light. Faith is like money. Without money, you can't purchase anything. And without faith, we can't expect healing.

If we are willing to have faith in God, He can heal. The Roman centurion believed in Jesus, and his faith led to the miracle. Jesus said to the centurion, *"'Go! Let it be done just as you believed it would.' And his servant was healed at that moment"* (Matthew 8:13b). In this story, God's word healed the servant.

Many years ago, I worked for a company and made many friendships there. In particular, I became friends with a male co-worker, and just by talking with him, we learned that both of us were Christians and loved Jesus. Because of our shared faith, one day he asked me to come to his church to teach the young people about science and God, because I was a pastor and had a degree from the University of Toronto in science.

This co-worker also shared with me that his wife was suffering from sciatica pain in her back. The pain was very strong, and she was on medication. She would need surgery to relieve the pain. I told my co-worker that I would keep her in my prayers.

Some time passed, and I went to my co-worker's church to conduct the seminar on science and faith. We had a wonderful session talking about how science doesn't oppose faith but rather affirms that there is a God who created things with order and wonder.

After the seminar, I felt a strong prompting from God to pray for my co-worker's wife. God told me, "Go into the sanctuary, lay hands on her, and pray for her." In my mind, I thought, *God, I can't pray for her. She'll think I am weird. I am not going to do it.* But God kept talking to me about praying for her. I hesitated because I'd just started in ministry, and to hear God speak to me like this was a new experience. I wondered if it was me talking to myself, or God talking to me. But the prompting was strong and didn't leave, so I decided to be obedient to God and asked my co-worker, "Can we go to the church sanctuary and pray at the altar for your wife?" Thankfully, he agreed. My co-worker, his wife, a few others, and I went to the sanctuary. My co-worker's wife knelt at the altar, and I laid hands on her and prayed, asking God to heal her.

The next week, my co-worker came by my desk. We talked about work, but then he informed me that his wife didn't have any pain anymore, and she had stopped taking her medication. I told him she should check with her doctor before discontinuing the medication. But I was in shock, and I asked my co-worker if he thought she had been healed. He wasn't sure, but he didn't rule out the possibility.

A few months later, he came by my desk to report that his wife had seen her doctor. The doctor explained that since she was pain-free, even while off medication, she no longer needed surgery. I couldn't believe it! I was ecstatic! I said to my co-worker, "I think God has healed her." He agreed and looked happy that his wife had been healed.

This healing started when I obeyed God's call to pray with my co-worker's wife. The Roman centurion said to Jesus, "Just say the word," and because of his faith in God's Word, his servant was healed. Never underestimate the power of God's Word in your life and the possibility of healing.

HEALED BY GOD'S TOUCH

Sometimes in the Bible people are healed by God's physical touch. In Mark 5, we read about a large crowd following Jesus. In the crowd was a woman who'd been bleeding for twelve years. She'd suffered greatly and had gone to many doctors. She'd spent all her money, but instead of getting better, she grew worse.

She'd heard about Jesus, so she came up behind Him and touched His cloak. She said to herself, *"If I just touch his clothes, I will be healed"* (Mark 5:28b). Immediately, the bleeding stopped, and she felt released from her suffering. Jesus realized that power had left Him, so He turned to the crowd and asked, *"Who touched my clothes?"* (Mark 5:30b). The disciples pointed out to Him the size of the crowd and wondered why He would ask that question.

Here is what the Bible says:

> But Jesus kept looking around to see who had done it. Then the woman, knowing what had happened to her, came and fell at his feet and, trembling with fear, told him the whole truth. He said

to her, "Daughter, your faith has healed you. Go in peace and be freed from your suffering." (Mark 5:32–34)

Why was she healed? The Bible says that her faith healed her. Her faith became her reality, and when she touched Jesus, she was freed from her suffering. She was healed by God's touch.

One year our church hosted a healing service for our congregation. We posted an ad in the local newspaper for people in our community to join us for that service. On that Sunday, a couple walked into our worship place. They had seen the ad, and the wife had wanted to come.

After I preached my message on healing, I invited people to step forward to be prayed for through the laying on of hands and the anointing of oil.

After I'd prayed over several individuals, I noticed that the visitor had stepped forward with her husband to our altar, where she began to explain her situation. She'd been diagnosed with a brain condition called Chiari malformation, and for several years had suffered with headaches and dizziness. She'd been scheduled for neurosurgery, but it was a high-risk operation, so it had been cancelled. She'd been waiting and resting for a year and had been unable to work for six months.

I asked her if she believed that God could heal her. She said yes, and we prayed together for healing. After that service, I never saw her again.

About a month later, she emailed me to tell me that she'd had an MRI and seen the neurosurgeon. The doctor couldn't believe the new MRI results. It showed that the affected part of the brain had returned to normal—without surgery. She said that she believed God had answered her prayers, and this was a demonstration of God's power in her life.

This testimony was a big deal for me because I was new in ministry and couldn't believe that God had worked in her body that way through our healing service. It not only encouraged me but it made me excited that indeed our God can heal. I shared her email with our church family and told them that God had heard our prayers and touched her body!

HEALED FOR GOD'S GLORY

What do you do when you want God to perform a miracle in your life, but you're dealing with a "dead" situation that can't be reversed? Can God still work in those situations? The answer is yes!

There's a story in the Bible about a man named Lazarus who becomes sick. He has two sisters, Mary and Martha, who send word to Jesus about his illness. When Jesus hears the news, He says that the sickness won't end in death but that God will be glorified.

Jesus loves Martha, Mary, and Lazarus, but He decides to wait two more days before going to see them. He even tells the disciples that Lazarus is asleep and that He'll wake him up (John 11:11). The disciples understand this to mean that he'll get better, but Jesus bluntly tells them that Lazarus is dead. He goes on to say that He's glad He wasn't there with Lazarus, because now they will believe. (This might seem like an odd thing for God to say, but He had a greater purpose in mind.)

When Jesus and the disciples arrive, Lazarus has been dead for four days. Martha comes to see Jesus and says that had He been there, her brother would still be alive (John 11:21). Jesus assures her that Lazarus will rise, and Martha agrees, thinking Jesus is referring to the last day (John 11:24). Jesus says to her, *"I am the resurrection and the life. The one who believes in me will live, even though they die; and whoever lives by believing in me will never die. Do you believe this?"* (John 11:25–26). Martha agrees with Jesus that He is the Christ and the Son of God.

Martha goes to get Mary, and together they take Jesus to Lazarus's tomb. Jesus tells them to take the stone away from the tomb, but Martha expresses concern over the odour that will be in there (John 11:39). Jesus responds with, *"Did I not tell you that if you believe, you will see the glory of God?"* (John 11:40b).

They roll the stone away, and Jesus looks up to God and thanks the Father for hearing His prayer, and then He says, *"… I said this for the benefit of the people standing here, that they may believe that you sent me"* (John 11:42b). Then Jesus calls out in a loud voice, "Lazarus!"

The dead man comes out, his hands and feet wrapped with linen and with a cloth around his face. Jesus tells the people to take off Lazarus's grave clothes and let him go.

We can imagine the grief and pain Martha, Mary, and the others felt. Their loved one had died! The death of a loved one is always a difficult, unbearable pain to experience. Both Martha and Mary pointed out to Jesus that had He been there, their brother would have lived. They wanted a healing, but God gave them something better—a resurrection.

Jesus said that this situation wouldn't end in death but would be an opportunity for people to believe in Him and see the glory of God. God had already determined the outcome, despite the ugliness of the situation. In bringing Lazarus back from the dead, God had a bigger purpose in mind—to foreshadow what would happen to Jesus. Jesus would die, but He would also rise. God used Lazarus's death to point people to Jesus.

Sometimes in life we face situations that we don't understand, and we ask God why it happened. I imagine that's how Mary and Martha felt. But God can use the hard situation we're going through to increase our faith in Him and for His glory.

• • •

> WE MAY NOT ALWAYS UNDERSTAND WHY
> WE'RE GOING THROUGH DIFFICULTY, AND WE
> MIGHT NOT LIKE IT, BUT WE CAN TRUST THAT
> GOD WILL ACCOMPLISH HIS PURPOSE.

• • •

The painful situation we're going through could be used to strengthen our faith or bring someone to faith in Jesus Christ. Our sickness could serve as a witness to another person.

The truth is, we don't know what God is doing because we can't understand the mind of God, but we can be certain that He's still working. Even when God doesn't answer our prayers the way we'd like Him to, we can always trust Him to use all situations for His glory and purpose. No matter what happens, God is good, and His purposes are good. All God asks is that we exercise faith in Him, even when it doesn't make sense.

HEALED THROUGH THANKFULNESS

In a culture that deems complaining as normal, we don't think about the power of thankfulness. But in Luke 17, we read a story about God completely healing someone because of faith and thankfulness.

Jesus was moving east to west from Samaria to Galilee, and on His way, He encountered ten men with leprosy. In those days, anyone with leprosy was deemed unclean (Leviticus 13–14). The ten lepers called out to Jesus and got His attention. They said, *"Jesus, Master, have pity on us!"* (Luke 17:13b). When Jesus saw them, He said, *"Go, show yourselves to the priests"* (Luke 17:14b). And as they went, they were cleansed, and all ten lepers were healed!

But the story doesn't end there. The Bible tells us that one of them came back to Jesus and *"... praising God in a loud voice ... threw himself at Jesus' feet and thanked him—and he was a Samaritan"* (Luke 17:15b–16). At this point, Jesus asked about the other nine.

How disappointing to read that only one cleansed leper came back to Jesus to praise Him. This man was also a Samaritan. Samaritans were Jews who observed different religious practices, and they were disliked by other Jews. The fact that Jesus even associated with the Samaritan is a big deal.

Then Jesus said to him, *"Rise and go; your faith has made you well"* (Luke 17:19b). In other translations, it says that his faith made him "whole." Jesus is saying that everything will be well. Why was this man healed completely and the others only received physical healing? All because of faith and thankfulness. This tells us that when we exercise both faith and an attitude of thankfulness to God, amazing things can happen in our lives!

This story reminds us that God doesn't just want to heal our bodies—He wants to deal with every broken situation in our lives. The man in the story was physically restored and left whole. God can do the same for us, but we have to believe and be thankful to God! When we do this, we can be made whole too!

During a particular season in my life, I began to suffer with pain in my back and leg. When I walked, I could feel nerve pain in my body. Initially, I thought, *I'm too young for this.* But health problems don't discriminate. You can face physical changes when you're young, middle-aged, or elderly. After researching my symptoms online, I was convinced that I had sciatica pain. I started doing stretches to alleviate my pain. They helped somewhat, but the pain was still present when I'd walk or sit.

It was a difficult time for me, because I needed to drive and visit people in the hospital or their homes, but I was in pain. One day I was praying to God and, just like this leper, I thanked and praised Him, despite my pain. I said, "Lord, I praise you for who you are, what you've done, what you've given to me. I thank you for my life, my home, my car, my family, my health." I walked in pain, but I praised and thanked the Lord.

I also asked God for healing: "Lord, heal me of this pain in my back and leg. If I'm in pain, how will I do my work? How will I prepare for Sunday morning sermons, preach, and visit the sick?" I also remember telling God, "You healed the lady with the sciatic pain at the altar. You asked me to pray for her when I went to her church, and she was healed. What about me?"

A few weeks later, after praying and doing my exercises, I noticed one day that the pain was gone! I knew God had touched my body and healed me! I was ecstatic! God had heard my prayers and answered!

My faith in God and my attitude of thankfulness were key to my healing. Many times I could have complained to God and grumbled, but like the leper who praised God, I chose to thank God despite my pain, and He chose to heal me.

HEALING IN JESUS'S NAME

When discussing faith and healing, it's important to think about the name of Jesus. His name isn't just any name—it has the power to do many things. That's why in Exodus 20, God tells the Israelites not to take His name in vain. God's name should be honoured, as it's powerful. In the New Testament, we learn that the name of Jesus is also powerful, and when used to heal someone, something amazing can happen.

In Acts 3, Peter and John are going to the temple for prayer. When they arrive, they see a man who's been lame from birth being carried to the temple gate called Beautiful. He was carried there daily to beg for money (Acts 3:2). When he sees Peter and John, he asks them for money. Peter says to him, *"Silver or gold I do not have, but what I do have I give you. In the name of Jesus Christ of Nazareth, walk"* (Acts 3:6b). Then Peter takes him by the right hand and helps him up, and the man's feet and ankles become strong.

The man walks into the temple courts and praises God. The onlookers remember that he is the same man who's been begging, and now he's walking. They're filled with wonder and amazement, and Peter asks them why they're surprised. He asks if they think human power or godliness made the man walk? Peter says to them, *"By faith in the name of Jesus, this man whom you see and know was made strong. It is Jesus' name and the faith that comes through him that has completely healed him, as you can all see"* (Acts 3:16b).

The key element to this man's healing was Peter's and John's faith in Jesus's name. They believed that this man could be healed, and that's what happened. We also can call upon His name and ask for healing, because the name of Jesus is powerful. The name of Jesus saves. The name of Jesus protects. The name of Jesus delivers because He is the One who died for our sins and rose on the third day. He defeated Satan and his evil plan. He forgives our sins and gives us new life in the Spirit. We can rejoice, because His name is power! God is still healing people today through faith in Jesus's name.

One Sunday after worship service, I was in an amazing mood. I was happy because someone in our church had donated five thousand dollars. For a church our size, that was a huge offering for one Sunday collection. God provided a blessing that day, so I was feeling excited about how He was working in our church.

Driving home, I was listening to worship music and giving God thanks. But then all of a sudden, I heard a noise. *Boom!* The car behind me hadn't stopped in time and rear-ended me.

I remember getting out of my car and, sure enough, I could see the damage to my car. After exchanging insurance information with the person at fault, I drove home, and that same night

I called my insurance company to file the accident report. I didn't have any physical pain that day, but the next day, I began to feel the effects of the accident. I had back, shoulder, and neck pain. I also was experiencing dizziness. As time went on, the dizziness got worse whenever I was on the computer or doing anything that stimulated my brain.

I had to take treatment three times a week, with two physio appointments and one massage appointment. I was upset about having to attend three appointments a week because during this time I was trying to complete my doctorate work. My final paper was due, and I was also working full-time as a pastor. Between the accident, work, and my paper writing, I was stressed, and the last thing I needed was a physically sick body.

I was given exercises to complete before and after my various rehab sessions. Sometimes the therapy helped, but other times it was painful. During that time, I would work on the computer, writing my doctorate paper or a sermon, but I'd have to stop every ten minutes and rest because my body was in pain and my head was spinning. Sometimes when I was driving, my neck would feel strained and I'd experience pain. At these times, I'd often say to God, "Why is this happening right now? You know I have work to do and a paper to complete."

Yet God was helping me and leading me through this journey of recovery. I continued going to therapy, and one of the things I did often was put my hand on the places that hurt and pray, "Jesus, please heal me." I would often say, "In Jesus's name."

My faith in God, and praying in Jesus's name, began to manifest, because my body started to change. Slowly but surely, God heard my prayer, and the dizziness and pain subsided and I felt strong again. I could do things like sit in my chair for an extended period of time, and drive and not have dizzy spells. My plea to God was working.

I persisted in faith, and about four months later, the therapists told me that I didn't need any further appointments. I was happy, and I know that God healed me because He can and because His name is powerful!

From these stories in the Bible and the experiences of myself and others, we see that healing is possible. In the Bible, when faith was present, God could do the impossible and heal individuals. I challenge you to think about yourself and others. If sickness is present, offer up your faith to God, trust in His will, and let God do His work. Just like He did for people in the Bible, God can heal you and turn your situation around.

Four

FAITH AND GOD'S PROVISION

WHEN WE PUT our faith in God, we must trust Him to provide for *all* our needs. This means we give up our right to control things and instead we say to God, "You are God and I am not." Even when things don't make sense, we trust that God will make a way in His time, His way, and using the resources He supplies for us. This is especially true when we go through seasons when our supply is short, but we must remember that God is not short of resources.

In the Bible, Paul reminds us of the truth that God can provide: *"And my God will meet all your needs according to the riches of his glory in Christ Jesus"* (Philippians 4:19). Another verse asks, *"Is anything too hard for the Lord?"* (Genesis 18:14a). In another place, Scripture tells us that we don't live by bread alone but by every word that comes out of the mouth of God (Deuteronomy 8:3). Over and over again, God proves that He can and will provide for our needs. Let's take a look at some biblical examples of God calling us to trust in Him.

FAITH, NOT WORRY

In Matthew 6, Jesus tells the people not to store up treasures on the earth but to store up treasures in heaven. Jesus is challenging the people not to put their purpose, security, and meaning of life in the riches of the world, or other people, but rather to focus on what God cares about first, and then He will take care of your needs.

In addition, Jesus shares that we shouldn't worry about life, as in what we will eat, drink, or wear. Life is more important than food, the body, and clothes. Even the birds of the air don't store up, but God the Father feeds them. Jesus explains that we are more important than the birds, and God will provide for our needs.

> If that is how God clothes the grass of the field, which is here today and tomorrow is thrown into the fire, will he not much more clothe you—you of little faith? So do not worry, saying, "What shall we eat?" or "What shall we drink?" or "What shall we wear?" For the pagans run after all these things, and your heavenly Father knows that you need them … Therefore do not worry about tomorrow, for tomorrow will worry about itself. Each day has enough trouble of its own. (Matthew 6:30–32, 34)

Jesus says that worrying accomplishes nothing except bringing stress in our lives. Yes, we should be concerned about situations, but God calls us not to worry. Instead of worrying, God calls us to have faith and trust in Him.

Many years ago, I had a conversation with my sister, and she asked me, "Why do we worry about things when God works it out?" This was a profound insight, and she was right. At times I've let my mind, emotions, and physical health suffer because I slipped into worry instead of trusting God. When I look back on those times, I can see that I let the fear of the unknown be the voice in my ear, not the gentle voice of God.

When I was in school writing my doctoral paper, I battled with worry because I was overwhelmed by the expectations, yet God kept telling me to trust Him. In the end, I completed the paper and the degree.

When I planted a church in 2008, I was overwhelmed with fear because I wasn't sure how the church was going to grow or connect with people in our community. As I write this paragraph, it has been fifteen years since our church began, and God has sustained and provided for us. In the end, God has proven to be faithful and loyal.

When the church was in a difficult financial situation, I worried sometimes rather than trusted in God. Again, God would come through, and we'd either receive a generous donation or we'd cut back in different ways to make the situation work.

All that time worrying accomplished nothing. That's why we should trust God and not worry. But we can get distracted, because at the end of the day, Jesus makes us think about this: Whom do we serve? Do we serve God or money? (Matthew 6:24).

When we have to have the "perfect" home, car, clothes, and life, we worry because we're putting our faith in earthly treasures, rather than in God. Jesus appeals to us to focus on what God cares about—the salvation of souls and people who need food, water, and clothing—rather than on earthly pleasures. When we do this, the Bible promises that God will take care of our needs: *"But seek first his kingdom and his righteousness, and all these things will be given to you as well"* (Matthew 6:33).

So what have you been worried about lately? Are you worried about being single? Becoming a parent? Your job? Your debt? Your family? Why not use that same physical, emotional, and mental energy on building your faith? When we do this, we replace the negative thoughts with ones that focus on God.

If we're consumed with earthly matters, we have a problem. If we make money more important than God, then we'll worry. Therefore, we need to shift our priorities. This will require a lifestyle change, and it will be a slow process for some people to get to where they need to be. But if we're patient and put God first, we'll be rewarded. We need to evaluate our life to check if we're placing God and His work first, particularly in the area of money. Review these questions:

1. What do you spend your money on?
2. Do you consume earthly things or the things of God?
3. Do you give generously to God and His work?
4. Do you spend more than you have?
5. Do you carry debt?
6. Do you track your finances to see what you're spending your money on?

Take the time to answer these questions. To see a change, you'll need to think about your money differently and develop disciplines in your life so that you exercise self-control over money, and money doesn't control you. Here are four things to think about regarding faith and money.

First, provision comes from God. When you think about your life, develop an appreciation for the fact that without God, you wouldn't have money, a job, material possessions, or your health. The Bible says that everything comes from God, and we only give what comes from His hand (1 Chronicles 29:14). When was the last time you realized that the only reason you have what you have is because of God?

Second, God wants you to give to Him in faith to learn to trust Him. Giving to God isn't about Him "needing" our money. God isn't broke. He is God! However, in the physical realm, money is what makes things happen or changes a situation. Giving to God is about us becoming more like Jesus.

In the Bible, two brothers who were raised by the same parents, in the same home environment, offered up two different offerings to God. Abel and Cain both brought an offering to God, but God had favour on Abel's offering versus Cain's offering. Why did God approve of Abel's and not Cain's? In Hebrews 11, we learn that *"By faith Abel brought God a better offering than Cain did. By faith he was commended as righteous, when God spoke well of his offerings"* (Hebrews 11:4a). Cain's offering was not right, because God said to him that if he did what was right, he'd be accepted. Abel's offering was by faith.

This is how God calls us to live. God provides for us, and then He calls us to give generously to Him and His cause. As we give to God in faith, we learn to trust Him with the little we have. Before we know it, God begins to bless our giving in ways beyond our imagination.

I learned this truth as I stepped into faith the first time I began to tithe. My older sister, Pramila, encouraged me and my twin sister, Tania, to give 10 per cent of our income to the Lord. At first I hesitated, because I was a student at university. However, after reflecting on what the Bible says and what my sister had communicated to me, I realized that I needed to give that 10 per cent to God.

Sunday morning arrived, and I sat in the service and watched the offering plate come down our aisle. I had my envelope and money ready for God. I was giving Him $50. I put the envelope in the offering and thought, *Well, God, I am trusting you as I put my 10 per cent in the offering plate.*

My mind couldn't prepare me for the financial blessing that was coming my way! During the next week, I received a notice in the mail that I was entitled to a $3,000 scholarship. I couldn't believe how God had taken my small $50 and multiplied it for His kingdom. God wants us to give to Him in faith.

Third, we give because we love God. Our motivation to give to God is fuelled by the grace of God. In the Bible, the Macedonian church gave because of the grace of God, *"They gave themselves first of all to the Lord, and then by the will of God also to us"* (2 Corinthians 8:5b). The Macedonian church was filled with the joy of God, and despite the severe trials they endured, they gave generously to Him. The Macedonians didn't use their situation as an excuse; rather, they gave out of love for God.

May that be our testimony as well—that we give generously to God because He gave to us first. God freely gave His Son, Jesus Christ, without hesitation, and because of His sacrifice for us, we have salvation. May we give to God because we are grateful for all that He has done.

When I was attending my home church in 2000, it was in the middle of a stewardship campaign. They challenged people to give because the church had a vision to expand and reach others for Jesus Christ. At the time, I was in university. The stewardship campaign details were shared with us, we were challenged in the sermons, and the complete vision was unveiled at a dinner at a banquet hall.

There was excitement surrounding the church, encouraging us to give generously to God for His kingdom and glory. We were asked to pray about how much to pledge to God.

The first campaign ran from 2000 to 2003. We were asked to give a three-year pledge. I pledged $50 a month, over and above my tithe. Three years passed, and I was able to tithe, pay my pledge, and pay my bills.

The second campaign ran between 2003 and 2006. This time I pledged $75. Again, I tithed, paid my pledge, and was able to pay my bills through my job.

The third campaign ran between 2006 to 2009. Again, I tithed and pledged for the Lord. The church conducted another campaign between 2009 and 2012, and I made a pledge to God and fulfilled my tithe to Him.

I am pleased to tell you that I was able to pay my tithe and my pledge in full, as well as all my bills. At the time I had to pay university school fees, and I needed to buy a car. Through it all, God provided me with a job. I disciplined myself financially and gave generously to God. I learned throughout this that I couldn't out-give God. More importantly, I gave out of love. God's love motivated me. I wanted to give back to God a small portion of what He'd given me.

Fourth, when you give to God, He wants to bless you. The Bible says in Malachi:

> "In tithes and offerings. You are under a curse—your whole nation—because you are robbing me. Bring the whole tithe into the storehouse, that there may be food in my house. Test me in this," says the Lord Almighty, "and see if I will not throw open the floodgates of heaven and pour out so much blessing that there will not be room enough to store it." (Malachi 3:8b-10)

God wants to bless us when we give. The blessing will come in different ways, but one of the ways He can bless is through money. We don't give to God because we want to be blessed, but we give generously to God as a by-product of His grace in our lives. In return, He sends money to bless us.

There's a radio station in our area that plays Christian music that I listen to regularly while driving. Every year they have an annual share-a-thon to raise funds to maintain the radio station. Every so often, they give updates on how much money they've raised and their monthly pledges. During their annual campaign, they ask listeners to be more than a listener but to give toward their mission.

Sometimes when I'd hear this, I'd feel convicted to give to the station, but I had every excuse in the book not to give: "God this just isn't the right time. I have other bills to pay. They don't need my money, and someone else will donate." But deep down I knew that God wanted me to pledge to the radio station because I often was blessed by listening to it. Finally, one day I decided to give. I made an online donation with my credit card for $100, in faith. As soon as I pledged, I felt good about my decision, because I knew I was being obedient to God.

Interestingly, during that same week, I was asked to teach a course to some of our denomination's pastors. I was asked to talk about mission and vision. I said yes to this opportunity and planned my lesson. I remember it as a wonderful time teaching and being with the students.

After teaching the class, the director of the program gave me a thank-you card. When I finally got home and opened the card, not only was there a note inside, but there was also $250 for my time and gas. I was thrilled. God took my $100 and made it $250 because I obeyed His voice and gave it to Him in faith.

This story shows how one act of obedience opened a door for me. God is looking to honour the person who gives in faith. He doesn't want us to make excuses for not giving, but He wants us to step out in faith and give to Him.

Do you need to prioritize giving so that you can experience the blessings of God? The Bible says to seek first His kingdom and His righteousness, and all these things will be given unto you (Matthew 6:33). As you seek His kingdom, you will see His hand move in your life in so many different ways that it will blow your mind. As you take care of God's business, God takes care of your business. Putting God first will help you to not worry but rather have faith in God, who will provide for you.

GOD CAN MULTIPLY

Sometimes we're in a dire situation and need God to perform a miracle for us right away, because if He doesn't, something drastic will happen: you might lose your job, your home, and in some cases, your life. Have you ever had to go through a situation like that? In the Bible, this was the situation for a woman in 2 Kings.

In the story, she cried out to Elisha (a prophet), telling him that her husband was dead. He had served and respected God, but now the creditors were coming to take her two boys as slaves (2 Kings 4:1). Her situation was not good—it was bad.

The prophet Elisha responded and asked, *"How can I help you? Tell me, what do you have in your house?"* (2 Kings 4:2a). Seems like an odd question, but she said that all she had was a small jar of olive oil. Elisha told her to go to all her neighbours and ask for their empty jars, and not just to ask for a few. After collecting the jars, she was to take them into her home and shut the doors behind herself and her sons. Elisha further instructed her to pour the oil into all the jars, and as each was filled, to put it to the one side.

The woman followed Elisha's instructions, and when all the jars were full, she told her son to bring her another jar. *"But he replied, 'There is not a jar left.' Then the oil stopped flowing"* (2 Kings 4:6b). The woman told this to Elisha, and he told her to pay her debt and that she and her sons could live off what was left over.

This is an amazing story of how God took a little oil and multiplied it! Elisha's instructions might have seemed odd, but it worked. Why? Because Elisha was a man of God and was in tune with God's voice. In the end, the word from Elisha came true. She paid off her debt, kept her boys, and had additional funds.

The woman's situation was impossible, but God was able to provide for her needs through His power and strength. God took the little she had and multiplied it for her good.

In 2013, Rosewood Church of the Nazarene, the mother church of the church plant I served in, Solid Rock Community Church of the Nazarene, was advertising a trip to Egypt, Jordan, and Israel for that fall. Rosewood hosted an information session in February 2013. The senior pastor was going to be away, so he asked me to attend the session to ensure that the projector, sound, and PowerPoint worked.

That night, the president of the travel company welcomed everyone to the session and then began to click through the slides of where they would be visiting, and he explained the biblical significance of each location. As I sat there, something in my heart began to stir, and I had a desire to go on the trip. But at the same time, I felt conflicted, because I was working on my doctorate during that season in my life. I wanted to travel to Egypt, Jordan, and Israel, but I was unsure of the cost and how I'd be able to cover it.

After the president finished his presentation, I was convinced that I was to go on the trip, but the financial details were still pending. I went home that night and said to God, "I know you're telling me that I'm going on this trip, but Lord, you'll have to show me how to pay for it." And then I left it in His hands.

Between February and June of that same year, the Lord provided two financial blessings. The first occurred in February 2013, when I learned that I was eligible to receive $3,000 for my education. The second came in June 2013, when I received a second scholarship for $1,500. In 2013, I received a total of $4,500 in

35

scholarships. This was more than enough to pay for my trip to Egypt, Jordan, and Israel.

God set me up to attend the information session. He put a desire in my heart to go on that spiritual journey, and He made a way for me financially. Everything was possible through the hand of God. What started as an impossible journey later became a testimony story I tell others about travelling to the Holy Land. The Lord multiplied the money through my circumstances. I had nothing to start with but ended up with $4,500.

That's how God works in our situations. He can bring something forward even if we have nothing or little in our hands. For the woman in the story, it was her jars and oil; for me, it was scholarships. God can use whatever He needs to multiply something in your life.

• • •

GOD IS CALLING US TO TRUST HIM NO MATTER WHAT SITUATION WE FACE. HE CAN PROVIDE, BECAUSE THAT IS WHO HE IS!

• • •

THE POWER OF THANKFULNESS

We have a family tradition at Thanksgiving in which we ask everyone to share what they're thankful for. One by one we listen to the stories of the blessings of God throughout the year, and we feel God's presence as we share how He's worked and who and what we're thankful for. This attitude of thankfulness coupled with faith is a powerful spiritual weapon we can exercise as we faithfully trust God to help us and provide breakthroughs in our lives. We often don't think about it, but in the Bible, faith and thanksgiving are very powerful together.

FAITH CAN MOVE MOUNTAINS

In Matthew 14, Jesus is with a crowd of people and asks the disciples to feed them. The disciples tell Jesus that they don't have enough food and to send the crowd away. But Jesus tells them again to feed them. The disciples explain that they have five loaves of bread and two fish. Jesus tells the people to sit down. *"Taking the five loaves and the two fish and looking up to heaven, he gave thanks and broke the loaves. Then he gave them to the disciples, and the disciples gave them to the people"* (Matthew 14:19b).

I had heard this story many times but only made the connection one day when I was preparing a message for Thanksgiving. The key moment in this passage occurs when Jesus takes the bread and fish and prays and gives thanks. He had an attitude of thankfulness, and because of this, the Word of God says that everyone ate.

The miracle of the story is that everyone had something to eat, but the other miracle was that they had twelve baskets of food left over. The number of men who ate was five thousand, but that doesn't include the women and children. This means there were more than five thousand people present and fed.

What started as an impossible situation became a possible situation for Jesus, the disciples, and the crowd. In reality, two fish and five loaves do not equal five-thousand-plus people fed. But because of prayer, thanksgiving, and faith, the math gets reversed.

If you're in a situation right now that looks impossible, have faith and give God thanks! Perhaps you have a friend or loved one struggling with an addiction. Maybe you're waiting for your financial breakthrough, for God to heal you, for God to send you a spouse, or you're trying to find a job. No matter the situation, let's be like Jesus. Have faith but also give thanks to God before the breakthrough. Before the miracle happened for this crowd, Jesus prayed, stepped out in faith, and gave thanks. I believe that we would see more breakthroughs in our life if we had an attitude of thanksgiving to God. What area in your life could you start to thank God for, even though the miracle hasn't happened yet?

From May 2019 to May 2020, my work income was reduced, and I had to adjust my lifestyle. Even though the situation was hard, during that season I prayed, "I don't understand the season I'm in, but I'm going to thank you. Thank you for my hours, my ministry, my health, my family." I was exercising what the Bible says, which is to give thanks in all situations (1 Thessalonians 5:18).

One day my sister called me to tell me that she and her husband were travelling to Niagara Falls and the Niagara Outlet, and she asked me to join them. At first I said no, because it was a two-hour drive from our home. But they wanted me to join them on this trip, so I agreed and they picked me up at my house. First, we'd go to the Niagara Outlet and then visit Niagara Falls.

Unfortunately, due to the time and traffic, our two-hour drive became three hours. When we finally arrived at the Niagara Outlet, I was exhausted. I wanted to go home because it was hot and I was tired. Eventually, we pulled into the parking lot and I gathered my belongings to get out of the car. As I was walking to the stores, I noticed a green paper on the pavement flashing in the sun. I wasn't sure what it was, but then my heart started to race. It was money. Two green twenty-dollar bills.

I picked them up and ran back to the car and told my sister. At first she didn't believe me, but then she saw the money in my hands and was shocked.

I looked around the parking lot again and saw another twenty-dollar bill, so I ran over and picked it up. I now had sixty dollars! By now, my brother-in-law had jumped out of the car and was running around the parking lot. He found a twenty, ten, and five-dollar bill—thirty-five dollars!

We were so excited! We huddled together as we held the money in our hands and wondered if someone had dropped their money or if it had fallen from the sky from God! Am I being illogical for saying that the money fell from the sky? I don't think so. Finding money from the sky, from God, is possible because God's Word says that every day the Israelites would wake up to manna, bread from heaven (Exodus 16:35). Even though we found the money, we wanted to make sure the money didn't belong to someone who'd dropped it, so we scanned the parking lot to see if anyone was looking for their money or a missing wallet. We didn't see anyone pacing the parking lot, so we waited a while before we started our shopping excursion. We wanted to be present if someone was missing the money, but no one claimed it.

As we began to walk to the stores, my brother-in-law said to me, "God sent you that money, Tina, because He knows you're on reduced hours."

I began to think about what he'd said, and I realized it could be true. I'm generally not the kind of person who finds money, and it was interesting that I found sixty dollars that day. In the end, I didn't spend it but put it in the bank. It was a blessing to find the money, but I believe that God heard my thankful heart during my difficult season and allowed me to experience this miracle in my life. It was God's way of telling me, "I heard your cry of thankfulness, and I will provide. You just have to trust me!"

SOMETIMES IT'S ABOUT GOD

Sometimes instead of God answering your prayer for a breakthrough, you'll find your resources becoming scarce. You're running low—low on cash, low on patience, or low on ways out of your situation. It might make you wonder if God can still work in situations where things are becoming scarce, and your anxiety is going up. The answer is yes! Sometimes God is allowing us to go through difficulties because He wants us to know that He alone is our provider.

A story in Judges 7 teaches us what to do if our resources are running low and why we can trust God. A man named Gideon was told by God that he had too many men with him to fight against the Midianites. The reason: God didn't want Israel to say that they'd saved themselves and take credit for winning the battle. Therefore, the Lord instructed Gideon to announce to the army, *"Anyone who trembles with fear may turn back and leave Mount Gilead"* (Judges 7:3b). Interestingly, 22,000 men turned back, which means only 10,000 men remained with Gideon.

Still, God thought there were too many men, so He told Gideon to take the remaining men to the water. When they got there, God told Gideon to separate the men who lapped the water with their tongues, like dogs, from those who knelt down to drink (Judges 7:5–6). Three hundred men lapped the water, while the rest drank by kneeling. The Lord confirmed to Gideon that the three hundred men who lapped the water would win the battle against the Midianites, and the rest were free to go home.

Again, why did God want only three hundred men to fight in the battle? Because He didn't want Gideon and the men to take credit for the victory. God wanted the Israelites to give the credit to Him. At first glance, this doesn't make sense, but it made perfect sense to God. He had a purpose in all of it: "You will not take credit for winning this battle; therefore, I will make you win with fewer men."

Often in our walk with God, what He asks of us doesn't make sense. In those moments, God doesn't want us to question Him but to trust Him. Trust that God will provide, heal, send help, fix the court battle, provide money, and resolve a broken relationship. Whatever you're going through right now might not be about you but about God. It's about God getting the credit in the end. We just need to sit still and let God fight our battles.

In 2017, my accountant noticed that I hadn't filed money I could have claimed on my 2015 tax file. My accountant told me to file this claim because it was over a thousand dollars. I agreed to file for the money, and my accountant drafted the letter asking for my 2015 tax file to be amended.

We sent the letter of amendment in the mail in 2017, but about two months later, we received a letter denying the amendment. My accountant reviewed the letter of denial and sent another letter, explaining the situation. This was in 2018, but once again, we received a denial letter. I was getting frustrated with how long it was taking to resolve this issue; however, my accountant didn't give up. We contacted the government, and the person on the phone explained that we needed to send an amended T4 (a statement of employment income and taxes) to receive the funds.

It was early 2019 when we sent the third letter. I wasn't optimistic that it was going to work, and I was tired of battling with the government for the past two years. During that time, as I spent time with God and prayed about the situation, I received a clear word from God: "You will receive the money this year." I don't know how to explain it, but that's what I heard God say to me clearly and audibly. I told myself, "God has spoken, so I need to believe and trust." God gave me this word on April 16, 2019.

Also during that time, our church family was going through financial difficulty. I was praying about what we should do as a church to offset our finances. At the April board meeting, I proposed that starting in May, we should reduce my hours so that we could meet our financial obligations. The board decided to reduce my hours temporarily.

In late May 2019, I was travelling for both personal and work reasons. I first went to a wedding in Sacramento, California, and then to Denver, Colorado for work. In Colorado after our work session, I decided to go back to my room to relax and check my mail and my bank account on my iPad. I typed in my client card number and the password for my bank account and happily discovered that on May 30, 2019, the money I'd been waiting two years for had finally been deposited into my account!

I was ecstatic! I couldn't believe the money had finally arrived. That same day, I praised God, but I also asked Him why it had taken so long. In my spirit, I heard God explain that now was the time that I needed the money, not before. When I was working full-time, my financial needs were being met, but now on reduced hours, the money would really benefit me. Whoa! I sat in God's presence in awe, because He was right. With my hours reduced, the money came to me at the right time!

This is how God works. He sees our needs, hears our prayers, and does the right things at the right time. What I thought was a nightmare (letters of denial) was a set-up by God to grant me the money at the time I needed it most. But more importantly, God reminded me of this truth that day: He is in control, and what made no sense to me made perfect sense to God. It wasn't about the money. It was about trusting God and what He was doing.

Gideon and Israel didn't understand why God reduced the number of fighting men, but when they won their battle, they understood that God wanted the credit. I didn't understand everything God was doing through my tax situation, but in the end, He came through. He knew what He was doing. I just needed to trust Him. Whatever situation you're going through right now, remember to trust Him, because in the end, He can change it. And when He does, it will point you back to God and His power.

THE ANSWER BEFORE THE PROBLEM

What if all the time we spend worrying, all the sleepless nights, and all those days of crying before God are just distractions when He is asking us to have simple faith in Him? I know I have been there, and in the end, those things didn't help. They only made my mental, emotional, and physical health falter.

As believers in God, we must trust God in all matters, and we must believe that God can resolve our problem before it even arises. That's what a good God does. That's what a sovereign God does, and that's what a God who provides does. He sees the problem before it happens, but He has an answer, too: *"Before they call I will answer; and while they are still speaking I will hear"* (Isaiah 65:24).

We learn this truth as well from a story in the book of Genesis. Joseph was sold by his eleven brothers into slavery. His brothers were jealous of him because their father, Jacob, favoured Joseph over the other boys. Due to this tension in the family, they sold Joseph and he ended up in Egypt, where he was a slave until the age of thirty.

God had given Joseph a vision at a young age that he would be in a position of power and authority. Finally, after many years of going unnoticed in his surroundings, Joseph was elevated to second in command of Egypt, because he was the only one who could interpret Pharaoh's dreams. (Pharaoh was first in command.) God gave Joseph the gift of dream interpretation, and through that, he knew that a famine was coming in Egypt. First Egypt would have seven years of food abundance, and then they'd experience seven years of scarcity.

During the years of Egypt's famine, Joseph's brothers were sent by their father, Jacob, to Egypt to get food. They arrived in Egypt, and Joseph recognized them, but they didn't recognize him. Through a series of events, Joseph revealed himself to the brothers as the one they had sold into slavery. Joseph was reconciled with his brothers and his father.

Eventually, Joseph's father died. When this happened, the brothers thought that Joseph would hold a grudge against them, but the Bible records:

> But Joseph said to them, "Don't be afraid. Am I in the place of God? You intended to harm me, but God intended it for good to accomplish what is now being done, the saving of many lives. So then, don't be afraid. I will provide for you and your children." And he reassured them and spoke kindly to them. (Genesis 50:19–21)

Joseph understood that God had sent him in advance to prepare the way for his brothers and his people, the Israelites, so that they would have food. God sent the answer before the problem.

Sometimes when we're going through hardships, we don't understand why, but perhaps God is sending us or doing something in advance to deal with a later problem. If that's the case, then God does know what He's doing and does care about us.

The other day I was going through a box of cards. At first, I was going to take all the cards and throw them into the recycling box, but I decided to go through each card one by one. I made piles. The wedding cards were put in the wedding pile, and the thank you cards were put in the thank you pile. I picked up one card and opened it and forty dollars US dropped out of the card. What was this? Then I began to read the card and said to myself, "I remember this card." I remembered the gift the person had put in the card, and then I asked myself, "How did I forget about this card? And the money?"

I went on my phone to check my text message to the person who'd given it to me. It was dated September 23, 2018. I had sent the person a thank you text for the card and lovely gift, and told them I was going to use it when I travelled to the US.

Almost a year later, on September 12, 2019, I found the card and money. Somehow, I'd forgotten about it. Here's the strange thing: I don't usually forget things. I'd even said to myself when I got the card, "I'm travelling to the US, so I'll use the money when I get across the border."

When I found the card and money, I asked God why I'd forgotten about it. The answer was, "You didn't need the money last year, and you need it now." God knew my financial situation would change in advance, and He sent the provision before the time. Now was the time to remember. God used the card and money to remind me that He knows what I need and He will provide.

God is all about provision. On the days I thought I wasn't going to make it, I did. When it seemed like there was no way, somehow God made a way. When I've been thankful, God has shown up. When I thought I was running out of resources, God proved that His arm isn't too short. When I thought God didn't know what He was doing, He always put me in my place to remind me that He is God and I am not. God sees all things, and as we step in faith with Him, He will provide.

Five

FAITH AND ACTION

HAVE YOU EVER had to deal with someone who needed your help? You know who I'm talking about. These are the people you listened to as they shared their problem. They cried to you over the phone. They complained about their life. After all the listening, crying, and complaining, you gave them advice, but then they didn't do anything with it! Instead of changing, they continued to do things their way.

Well, my friends, this can happen in our faith journey with God. There's nothing sadder than believing in God but not doing anything with our faith. We have a phrase for people who are like this: "all talk but no action." If we believe there is a God, then our lives must reflect that. Our faith must be visible. People should see evidence of our faith based on how we think, talk, behave, and feel.

James writes about faith and action in his letter to the church. He said, *"What good is it, my brothers and sisters, if someone claims to have faith but has no deeds? Can such faith save them?"* (James 2:14). James says it's no good to have faith but no action. *"In the same way, faith by itself, if it is not accompanied by action, is dead"*

(James 2:17). Therefore, faith should produce action in our life. What kind of tangible, noticeable, clear actions should our faith in God produce? Here are a few:

FAITH CAUSES US TO LOVE

If we say we believe in God and love Him, but we don't show through our actions that we love others, then perhaps we model a *false* faith. James further describes faith without actions this way: *"Suppose a brother or a sister is without clothes and daily food. If one of you says to them, 'Go in peace; keep warm and well fed,' but does nothing about their physical needs, what good is it?"* (James 2:15–16) James is right. How can we say we love God and have faith in Him if we don't care about the brother or sister who needs our help? Faith must drive us to love. We must be willing to show love to others for our faith to be substantiated.

Recently, three of our ladies in our church district became ill. One day I thought, *We should send them a card.* I asked our women's leader if we could send a card to their houses to encourage them, and she was excited and said yes! I took the time to write the cards, go to the post office, and mail them. After placing the cards in the mailbox, I smiled. I was excited about them opening the cards and seeing that despite their health challenges, our women in our church district loved them and, more importantly, God loved them too!

Loving someone doesn't have to be hard, but somehow we've made it difficult. There are so many simple ways that our faith can drive us to love. We can call someone, send them money, visit them, donate clothes or food, send someone a card or a gift. We can babysit for busy parents or take people to their appointments. The list goes on. Faith should cause us to love. When you think about your life, can you say that your faith is driving you to love? Is your faith producing action?

FAITH DRIVES US TO OBEDIENCE

In that same chapter, James asks if his readers want more evidence that faith without works is useless. He refers to Abraham in Genesis 22, when God called him to sacrifice his son.

> You foolish person, do you want evidence that faith without deeds is useless? Was not our father Abraham considered righteous for what he did when he offered his son Isaac on the altar? You see that his faith and his actions were working together, and his faith was made complete by what he did. (James 2:20–22)

James refers to Abraham because when God called him to sacrifice his son, it was no small matter. Abraham had waited a long time for Isaac, the son he had with Sarah, and now God was asking him to give him up. That just didn't make any sense, yet Abraham obeyed. He took Isaac and prepared to kill him. Abraham was walking out his faith, willing to trust and obey God. He essentially was saying to God, "I don't understand, but I'm still going to trust you."

Can people say the same thing about our lives? Are we obeying God in faith, even when life doesn't make sense? What does faith in action look like? It looks like this: Someone we love dies, and we still attend church that same week and raise our hands and worship God. We lose our job, but we still give God our tithe and offering. Someone we love hurts us, and we forgive them, even though we didn't do anything wrong. We go through a separation and divorce, and we still serve in the church. We're tempted to do something wrong, but we make the hard choice and walk away, even though we might lose friends, family contacts, jobs, money, security, titles, or our significant others. When we do what God calls us to do no matter the cost, we put our faith in action! Can we say that we are exercising faith into action through obedience to God? Faith in action means that no matter what happens, I am going to trust God and obey Him.

FAITH LEADS US TO TRUST GOD WITH WHAT WE HAVE

When we walk out our faith in God, we must show others that real faith means trusting God no matter what season we're in. This means that we won't always be in a season of abundance, but whatever we do have, God wants us to use it and trust Him. In Mark 12, Jesus sees men coming and putting large sums of money in the offering. Then a poor widow comes and puts in two small copper coins, worth only a few cents. Jesus calls His disciples together and says to them, *"Truly I tell you, this poor widow has put more into the treasury than all the others. They all gave out of their wealth; but she, out of her poverty, put in everything—all she had to live on"* (Mark 12:43–44).

• • •

REAL FAITH MEANS WE TRUST GOD WITH WHAT WE HAVE AND THAT HE WILL WORK OUT ALL THE DETAILS OF OUR LIVES.

• • •

In one season of ministry, the church was in a challenging financial situation, so I told the leaders that we needed to cut expenses so that we could pay our bills. I suggested that we cut my salary by 25 per cent and pay off our deficit. We agreed and decided that this was a temporary solution. To be honest, I wasn't sure how I was going to pay all of my bills, but I can testify that throughout the year, God provided for me. He sent money in all sorts of ways.

During that time, I visited a man who was sick. I'd go to his house and read Scripture and pray with him. Unfortunately, he eventually died. When he passed away, I went to the funeral service to show my support to the family. The wife of the deceased appreciated my visits and support during such a difficult time, so she sent me a cheque for $250 for educational use. I remember getting the cheque and thinking, *Wow, God, you are amazing!*

That same year, I began helping my sister in event planning. I attended some of her events, and she paid me for my time. This was an additional income for me that year.

At other times I'd conduct services for families who needed help or requested it, and they would donate money for my time. God was working through all of these things, and at the end of the year, I'd made as much as I would have working full-time! I couldn't believe it, but that's how God works!

Even though my salary was reduced by a quarter, I chose to continue to give my tithes and offerings faithfully to God. I wanted to practise my faith in action, even though I was in a different season in my life. But through this season, God showed me that He was faithful and provided for me! I used what I had to bless God, and He blessed me in return.

Whatever you have, big or small, trust God with it. Continue to be faithful to God and put your faith in action. Do you have a little church, a little money, a little dream to start a business, a little house, or a little job? Whatever you think isn't enough *is* enough because your little, plus faith in God, is more than enough for God. Trust God with the little you have and He will make a way.

FAITH FOSTERS SPIRITUAL MATURITY
Faith in action also means that we're serious about growing in the Lord. When we give our hearts to Jesus, we make a choice to be intentional about growing in our walk with God. We must—no,

we need to—desire to be more like Jesus. In Romans 12:11, Paul writes, *"Never be lacking in zeal, but keep your spiritual fervor, serving the Lord."*

In order to grow, we need to spend time with God. How often do you spend time with God? Is God in your schedule? This can be an area of struggle for some people. Some people do everything on their to-do list first and then squeeze God into their schedule, but it's better to put God first—then you'll see how easy it is to get all the other things done.

If we're going to learn what's important to God, we need to sit before Him and spend time with Him. We'll never learn to be like Jesus if we don't make time for Him. Spending time with God needs to become a lifestyle, not a habit.

Here are some things we can do to increase our time with God and put this area of faith into action. First, find a place to spend time with God. Some people spend time with God in a closet, office, outside, or at their desk. It doesn't matter where you meet with God, just find a place to have a date together. I meet with God at my desk. When I was attending university, I met with God at my kitchen table. Wherever you choose to meet with God, make sure it's free of people, phones, computers, tablets, TV, radio, or anything else that will distract you.

Next, find a time to meet with God. The Bible says that Jesus would often spend time with God early in the morning, *"Very early in the morning, while it was still dark, Jesus got up, left the house and went off to a solitary place, where he prayed"* (Mark 1:35). You can also meet with God at night, *"One of those days Jesus went out to a mountainside to pray, and spent the night praying to God"* (Luke 6:12). Jesus demonstrates that you can meet with God in the morning and/or the evening.

Once you've set a place and time, you need to decide *how* you'll spend your time with God. During this time, you can read a chapter in the Bible or from a devotional. Spend time reflecting on what you've read. You can make notes in a journal or meditate on the Word. Ask yourself: What's going on in the passage? Who's involved? Where does the story take place? When does the story take place? How is God involved? While you make notes or reflect on God's Word, ask yourself this question: How does what I read impact my life? What changes do I need to make in my life to apply the Word?

Spend some time in worship and prayer, praising God for all the good things He has done and will do. Also, spend time praying about heavy burdens in your life and the lives of other people. This way you'll be mentioning them in your prayers and interceding for others. Worship can be simple: "Lord, thank you for who you are. Thank you for my family, and for this weather." Prayer can be simple: "Lord, help my marriage. Heal brother Jim; send money for sister Helen." If you're still shy about prayer, a good prayer to say every day is the Lord's Prayer:

> This, then, is how you should pray:
> "Our Father in heaven,
> hallowed be your name,
> your kingdom come,
> your will be done,
> on earth as it is in heaven.
> Give us today our daily bread.
> And forgive us our debts,
> as we also have forgiven our debtors.
> And lead us not into temptation
> but deliver us from the evil one." (Matthew 6:9–13)

Jesus taught His disciples to say this prayer because it covers everything in life from praising God, to God's will, to asking for provision, to forgiving those who hurt us, to helping us overcome our temptations, and to delivering us from Satan and his schemes.

When you pray, sit in silence to hear from God. Sometimes we forget that prayer is a conversation with God. We talk, but then we need to listen to what God is saying about the matters in our lives. This will allow the Holy Spirit to speak into our lives and give us insight into what we should or should not do.

Putting our faith in action means we genuinely desire to grow in God. Why not begin to plan or build on your daily time with God and see Him enrich your life in so many ways?

FAITH MOTIVATES US TO SERVE AND USE OUR GIFTS FOR GOD

In a busy society, we want to serve God, but often our response is that we're just too busy. But if we pause and think about how we spend our time, we'll see that we might be spending it on things that don't have purpose—specifically, eternal value. This might mean we need to prioritize our time. That's why Paul writes in 2 Corinthians 4:18, *"So we fix our eyes not on what is seen, but on what is unseen, since what is seen is temporary, but what is unseen is eternal."*

Keep this verse in mind when you think about how you use your time. How much time in your week is devoted to yourself, other people, and miscellaneous things? Don't get me wrong—we have to take the time to drive our kids to school, buy groceries, attend worship services, etc. But many of the other hours in your day are just dead space, devoted to things that don't matter or have an eternal impact.

Faith in action means we use our gifts and time for God. Every believer in Jesus Christ has a spiritual gift or gifts. A spiritual gift is something you can do through the power of the Holy Spirit as He enables you to function in your gift. For example, I have the gift of teaching the Bible. Let's take a look at what the Bible says about gifts.

> For just as each of us has one body with many members, and these members do not all have the same function, so in Christ we, though many, form one body, and each member belongs to all the others. We have different gifts, according to the grace given to each of us. If your gift is prophesying, then prophesy in accordance with your faith; if it is serving, then serve; if it is teaching, then teach; if it is to encourage, then give encouragement; if it is giving, then give generously; if it is to lead, do it diligently; if it is to show mercy, do it cheerfully. (Romans 12:4–8)

This passage helps us understand spiritual gifts. We are one body with many members, which means many people make up the body of Christ, but we all have different roles. Some have the gift of prophesying, faith, serving, teaching, encouragement, giving, leading, or mercy. The goal for every believer is to discover their spiritual gift(s) and then use it for God.

For example, if you have the gift of mercy, you want to be involved in ministries like visiting the sick or being there for someone who's lost a loved one. If your gift is giving, then you want to be involved in encouraging others to donate to important matters. If your gift is faith, then you believe that God can provide and do the impossible in any situation.

Once you know what your gifts are, use them for God's glory. Don't sit back and let others use their gifts to bless you. You bless others with your gift. When you use your gift to bless others, you'll feel a sense of joy and blessing in your life.

Review the following questions:

1. What is your spiritual gift? If you don't know, then take a spiritual inventory test or meet with the pastor/leaders of your church to identify your gift.
2. Begin to use your gift for God. Take time to develop the gift so that you grow and become better at it, whether teaching, visiting, praying, etc.
3. Practise your gift regularly. Don't just use your gift one time, but on a regular basis.

There's a big world out there, and if each person does their part, the kingdom of God will grow and more people will come to know Jesus as their Saviour. It can start with you.

Faith in action means that I don't just believe in Jesus, but I am the hands and feet of Jesus. People see Jesus in me—in the way I talk, behave, think, dress, carry on my work, serve, and handle my money. There's a difference in me because Jesus is making me different. If we look like the rest of the world, then we won't be the salt and light God is calling us to be. We *must* be different so that others will see the light and eventually desire a relationship with the Light, Jesus Christ.

Six

FAITH AND BOLDNESS

ON A HOLIDAY in Antigua, some friends and I decided to go on a zip line as one of our excursions. I bravely signed up, and we completed the pre-training on how to use our harnesses. Now we were ready for the first drop.

I got in line, but as we got closer to the drop point, I started to get nervous. All of a sudden, what had looked exciting and exhilarating became dreadful as each person was released and sent across to the other side. I started to breathe more heavily and could feel my body begin to tighten. I tried to find a way to get out of line, but it wasn't easy because there were people behind me—plus, I'd already bought my ticket.

So I did what I had to do. I exercised courage and faith that God would help me through the situation, and that's exactly what happened. I stepped up to the line. The zip line workers spoke to me, and then released me into the air. As I flew across to the other side, I looked down. I could see God's creation from an amazing angle, but I'm not going to lie to you—I did it with fear. At the end of the excursion, they gave us a certificate congratulating us for completing the event and exercising faith. I couldn't believe they used the word "faith," but there it was on my certificate.

In our walk with God, sometimes we need to exercise what I call bold faith.

• • •

BOLD FAITH IS STEPPING OUT OF OUR COMFORT ZONE EVEN THOUGH WE'RE SCARED

• • •

—just like I had to do with my zip lining experience. Because of fear, we don't always step out in faith. Fear might be why we don't apply for a job or a school program, or why we don't give dating a chance. Deep down inside, all of us fear rejection. We don't like the feeling of failure and its impact on our confidence. But if we want to see God move in our lives, we have to face our fears and step out. It won't be easy, but it can be done. There are examples in the Bible of what bold faith looks like and what we should expect when we exercise it.

YOU WILL GO ALONE

Sometimes when we start to do what God calls us to do and step out with bold faith, we have to go forward alone. If you like to always have company, or you get energized by crowds, this will be hard for you. But whatever God is asking you to do, you can do it, and you can do it alone.

In Matthew 14, Jesus tells the disciples to go into a boat ahead of Him. While they're in the boat, Jesus goes to the mountain to pray. When evening comes, Jesus is alone, and the boat is now a far distance from the land. The wind and waves are against it, and that night Jesus goes out to the disciples by walking on the lake.

When the disciples see Jesus, they're scared and think that He's a ghost. Jesus says to them, *"Take courage! It is I. Don't be afraid"* (Matthew 14:27b).

Peter then takes a step of faith:

> "Lord, if it's you," Peter replied, "tell me to come to you on the water."
> "Come," he said.
> Then Peter got down out of the boat, walked on the water and came toward Jesus." (Matthew 14:28–29)

Out of the twelve disciples, Peter was the only one who stepped out of the boat. Think about this for a moment. There were twelve men, but only one had the faith to walk on the water. Mathematically, this means that less than 10 per cent of the men in the boat were willing to step out in faith. But this is what bold faith looks like. You will have to go alone. Sometimes, you and I will be the only ones willing to do what God wants us to do.

Maybe you're the only one who will complete your education, purchase a house, get married, survive sickness, write a book, or work in a ministry for God. Whatever the case may be, it all starts with bold faith.

What opportunities are you missing because of fear? Because you don't want to go alone? I'm sure that when you look back on your life, you'll regret some things and wish you'd acted in faith and trusted in God, because now you'd be reaping the benefits of bold faith. But instead, you might have let fear take over. Don't let it stop you now. Overcome whatever you were afraid about in the past. Choose to have bold faith, even if you have to go alone.

IT WON'T ALWAYS MAKE SENSE

Bold faith sometimes means you'll have to do what God asks of you, even though it doesn't make sense. It might be contrary to your thinking or your usual way of doing things. It will make you uncomfortable, and you'll worry about what others think. But God is asking you to do it. You'll have to make a choice to trust God and do it or completely go in the other direction.

This was the case for a man named Naaman. Naaman was the field marshal of the king of Aram. He was great—a hero—and he received victory from God. Although he was a valiant soldier, he faced a challenge—he had leprosy (2 Kings 5:1). There was a stigma attached to a person with leprosy because they would have had scales and blotches on their skin, turning it white. Although life looked good for Naaman, on the inside, he carried this deep burden.

Naaman was also an Aramean, which meant he was an enemy of the Israelites. In the story, he takes the Israelites captive, including a young lady who was a servant to Naaman's wife. She told Naaman's wife that there was a prophet in Samaria, Elisha, who could cure him of his sickness.

Naaman told the King of Aram about this, and the king allowed him to go and see the prophet. King Aram contacted the Israelite king through a letter, and Naaman prepared a large gift to establish a relationship with the Israelite king; however, the Israelite king mistook the letter as an act of war, thinking the Aramean king wanted to start trouble with him.

In the end, Elisha, the prophet of God, heard about the situation and sent a message to the King of Israel, summoning Naaman to himself. Naaman went with his horses and chariots and stopped in front of Elisha's door. The Bible says, *"Elisha sent a messenger to say to him, 'Go, wash yourself seven times in the Jordan, and your flesh will be restored and you will be cleansed'"* (2 Kings 5:10).

Naaman got mad at Elisha and started to complain. He wanted the prophet to come down, wave his hand, and call on his God to cleanse Naaman. Naaman didn't like this solution to his problem because it didn't make sense, but he went to the Jordan anyway and dipped himself in seven times. When he did, his body was restored!

Sometimes God will tell you what you need to do, but it's going to take faith and it won't make sense. What God tells you might be crazy and illogical. Sometimes we say to God, "Lord, you want me to do what?" For example, "Lord, you want me to donate all this money to this person? God, you want me to have children when I'm over thirty-five years old? God, you want me to pray for my children, and in due time they will turn around? You want me to keep this job and not apply to another one with a higher salary?"

The Bible is filled with stories of God asking people to do something that made no sense. He asked Hosea to marry Gomer, a prostitute—that didn't make any sense. When God asked Joshua and the people to walk around the walls of Jericho seven times, that didn't make sense. When God asked Abraham to take his son, Isaac, and sacrifice him, that didn't make sense. Sometimes God will tell us to do things that don't make any sense to us, but here's the key: trust God and do it anyway. Have bold faith. Is there something in your life right now that God has been asking you to do, but you don't want to do? My advice is to have bold faith and do it anyway.

BE THE FIRST

Sometimes having bold faith in God means trusting God and His Word and being the first one to do what no one else has done. This means you'll have no reference point. You can't talk to someone about what they did, or read up in a history book about how to resolve what God is asking you to do, because you'll be the first doing it. Although it's scary, go ahead and do it, because God is asking you to.

Noah lived in a time when the people who occupied the land were displeasing in the eyes of God. Humanity was wicked, and the *"inclination of the thoughts of the human heart was only evil all the time"* (Genesis 6:5). Humanity was in moral decline, and God was grieved that He'd made them. God felt sorrow at humanity's behaviour.

But amid the evil in the world, there was a man with whom God was pleased, and his name was Noah. The Bible describes him as someone who found favour with God. He was righteous, blameless, and walked with God (Genesis 6:8–10). Noah was set apart from the rest of the world, and God planned to destroy the entire world because it was corrupt. God said to Noah, *"I am going to put an end to all people, for the earth is filled with violence because of them. I am surely going to destroy both them and the earth"* (Genesis 6:13b).

God wanted to spare Noah and his loved ones, so He asked him to build a boat. This boat was to be bigger than regular boats because it would need to hold humans as well as animals. God instructed Noah to bring two of every living creature, male and female.

The Bible says, *"Noah did everything just as God commanded him"* (Genesis 6:22). Noah believed and trusted everything God said He was going to do. Up to this point in the book of Genesis, the people had never experienced rain. God was going to bring floodwaters, and Noah trusted God's word. Noah didn't question God or ignore His command. Noah built the ark.

The flood did destroy the world, except for Noah and his family and the animals in the ark. But this is an important question: Did everyone believe like Noah? Did everyone put their trust in

God while Noah was building the ark? No. In Luke 17:27, Jesus says, *"People were eating, drinking, marrying and being given in marriage up to the day Noah entered the ark. Then the flood came and destroyed them all."* Some people ignored what God had told Noah and lived their lives the way they pleased.

Noah reminds us that exercising bold faith means you have to trust God even if others ignore what He has said to you. Sometimes it means you'll be the first one to do what He asks.

Noah didn't have a blueprint on how to prepare for a flood. He was the *first* one to do something like this in his generation. Sometimes you'll be the first one. For example, you might be the first in your family to follow God, even though others choose to reject the gospel. You might be the first to agree with God about something He's told you about your spouse, children, job, health, finances, or relationships. You might be the first to do what's right even though it's not popular.

When I felt called to ministry, some people in my life didn't understand why at twenty-three years of age I was switching from a science degree to a religious studies degree. Thankfully my family supported my calling to be a pastor, and the church I was attending gave me a reference when I applied for my new program. I was accepted into it and began work on my Master of Divinity.

After completing that degree, God called me to plant a church, which I did with the support of our mother church and others in September 2008. Although my life took a different turn than what I'd expected, I exercised bold faith. I was the first in my family to become a pastor. We'd had no other pastors in our family. And I'm a female pastor! But that is what bold faith means—taking God at His word and being the first one to do something that hasn't been done before. Will you be the first one in your family, circle, neighbourhood, or country to do something great for God?

THERE WILL BE A COST AND A REWARD

When we exercise bold faith, there will be a cost and a reward. That's the nature of life—you put one foot forward but have to deal with the pushback of moving ahead. Nobody gets to be a professional athlete without putting in the practice time. You can't get an education degree without studying and writing assignments. You don't become the president of a country without talking to and influencing people. Every great thing in life requires time, energy, and investment. There is a cost. The same is true with bold faith. But in the end, it's worth it.

In the book of Esther, the Persian King Xerxes gives a royal banquet and displays his wealth and power. His queen, Vashti, refuses to attend the banquet, so the king banishes her and begins the search for a new queen. Esther, a poor, young Jewish woman who enters the court, is chosen among all the other ladies because of her great beauty.

In the backdrop of this book, tension arises when a man named Haman, second in command to King Xerxes, develops hatred toward one of Esther's relatives, Mordecai, and the Jewish people. Haman plots to kill Mordecai and the Jews, and he convinces King Xerxes to issue a decree to have the Jews destroyed. When Mordecai discovers this, he's devastated, and so are the Jewish people.

There is wailing and mourning among the Jews. Mordecai sends word back to Esther and explains the danger they are all in. He suggests to her that she might have come into her royal position for that very season (Esther 4:14). Mordecai is saying that maybe God allowed Esther to be queen so that she could influence the king and bring deliverance to the Jews. Esther responds to Mordecai by saying:

> Go, gather together all the Jews who are in Susa, and fast for me. Do not eat or drink for three days,

night or day. I and my attendants will fast as you do. When this is done, I will go to the king, even though it is against the law. And if I perish, I perish. (Esther 4:15–16)

Pay attention to the fact that Esther said she would go to the king even though it was against the law. Back in those days, no one could go to the king unless the king asked for that person. Esther decided to risk her life and go to him anyway. That's what it means to have bold faith. She didn't know how it was going to work out for her, but she knew the cost could be her life. But if the king listened to her, then she could spare her people.

This is how people with bold faith act—they're always keeping the result in mind. They're always thinking about the positive things that can come about if they stick it through or take that leap of faith. People with bold faith talk like this: "I'm glad I kept my faith, because now my marriage is where it needs to be. I'm glad I didn't give up on my child but instead exercised faith, because he or she made it. I'm glad I kept working hard, because now I have a degree. I'm glad I took the extra courses for work, because I was promoted or still have my job."

When we exercise bold faith in God, there will be a cost but also a reward. What would happen if we exercised bold faith in our homes, schools, churches, communities, countries, and the world? I dare to think that the world would be a different place.

Seven

CORPORATE FAITH

THE FIRST TIME I went to Egypt, Jordan, and Israel with a tour group, it was an amazing experience. I saw the places that brought the Bible alive for me, like where Jesus prayed in the Garden of Gethsemane, and where He preached the Sermon on the Mount. We also went to the Sea of Galilee, where Peter walked on water. Everything about the trip was great, but I regretted that I didn't have anyone close to me to share my experience with. Everyone else on the trip had a family member or friend with them, but I didn't have anyone. After the trip, I said to myself, "If I ever go again, I'll bring someone I know."

Two years later, I went with a group of forty-five people to Rome, Egypt, Jordan, and Israel. This time, my dad, my brother-in-law, and a good friend came with me. The presence of people close to me on the trip made it even more special when we visited the biblical sites because we got to do it together!

It's the same with our faith in God. When we express and live out our faith in a community, it matters. I call this "corporate faith." There's just something about people coming together to experience the same thing at the same time. When you go to a sports game and thousands of people see the same play, doesn't it make your adrenaline skyrocket? Yes! Therefore, when two, ten, one hundred, or thousands of people come together and express faith in God, there is power. Let's look at what corporate faith means and how it can impact us.

IT MEANS WE AGREE

Corporate faith in God means we agree together. When you and I say that we're going to believe together, work together, and do life together, then God can do something beyond our expectations. But we won't see that if we don't agree. I believe that we are missing many amazing things in our lives simply because we dismiss the power of faith and agreement. In a world in which being individualistic and pursuing your dreams are praised, the Bible talks to us about the positive benefits and power of corporate faith and being in agreement.

In Joshua 24, Joshua rounds up the leaders, the officials, the judges, and the people of God after he hears from God. He tells them that long ago, their ancestors worshipped other gods. But God took Abraham and gave him Isaac. Isaac had Jacob, and Jacob and his people lived in Egypt. The Egyptians afflicted the Israelites, and God heard the cry of His people. God reminds them that when their enemies came against them, He spared them and brought them out and allowed them to cross into Jericho.

Then Joshua tells the people that they need to fear God, serve Him, and throw away their gods. If that seems undesirable, then that's their choice. But Joshua says to the people, "But as for me and my household, we will serve the Lord" (Joshua 24:15b). By saying this, he's making a public declaration to the people that his house will be in agreement and will not waver. They're not going to serve God today and change their minds tomorrow. They are going to *serve the Lord*. That's what corporate faith looks like. We are going in one direction, one way, and experiencing life together.

When there is no unity in faith among the people, there is trouble. That's why there's conflict around the world—because there's no agreement. North America operates like this. You do your thing, and I'll do my own thing. As long as we don't hurt each other, we're good. However, when we don't agree, there is chaos. What kind of chaos?

When as individuals we disagree with God, we'll see trouble in our lives because we make the wrong choices. We might lie, steal, be sexually impure, and become angry. We need to agree with God in order to see peace, blessings, and less pain in our lives. When we're not aligned with God, we'll align with something else. Where there's no agreement, there's no power.

In our marriages and families, if there's no agreement, there will be tension in the home. If couples can't agree on how to spend money, there will be a financial strain. If the home is spiritually in disarray, then there will be a split on church attendance or how to deal with situations. If children don't listen to their parents, there will be anger in the home. Where there is agreement, there is unity. Do you have agreement in your home?

What about the church community? Agreement means we'll show love to one another. Everyone will give generously to the cause of Christ and do their best to be present in worship, serving, praying, and reading God's Word. When this happens, there is an agreement!

Corporate faith in God means we choose to agree. Joshua challenged the people to agree on which God they would serve. In our walk with God, we need to agree with God and others so that we will move in the right direction.

IT CREATES A SPACE FOR MIRACLES TO HAPPEN

When God's people have corporate faith, miracles happen. Don't believe me? Let's look at the story of Jesus passing through Capernaum. Many people heard that He was in town, so they gathered to hear from Him. There were so many people there that there was no room left in the house.

While Jesus was preaching the Word, four men brought a paralytic to Him. Unfortunately, because so many people were in the room, the four men couldn't reach Jesus, so they made an opening in the roof above Jesus and then lowered the man, who was lying on his mat.

This is what God's Word says: *"When Jesus saw their faith, he said to the man, 'Take heart, son; your sins are forgiven'"* (Matthew 9:2b). God was interested in both the man's spiritual and physical healing. But notice what the Bible says: *"When Jesus saw their faith."* The corporate faith of the four friends moved Jesus to heal the man.

Do you have people in your life willing to do whatever it takes to see that you have a breakthrough? People who will fight with you during your battles and, more importantly, have *faith* like these men? This is what corporate faith looks like for the people of God—believing for something to happen for you and others.

It was the middle of the night, and I heard my phone vibrate. Normally, I turn vibrate off when I go to sleep, but ironically, I'd forgotten to put it on silent. It was a text from a friend: "If you're awake, please call me. It's an emergency."

I immediately called her. She informed me that her husband was very sick and was at the hospital. The situation was bad—really bad. She soon had to take another call, but I told her I'd be praying. There I was in my room, very concerned for my friend. I spent the next forty-five minutes on my knees, asking God to intervene. I also kept reading God's Word aloud. Looking back now, I know that God had ensured that I saw the text message so that I could pray and intercede for her husband.

The next day, many others were informed about her husband's condition and began to lift prayers to God. Digital prayer meetings were held for the man. One week passed. No improvement. Then about a week and a half later, he finally woke up. It was a miracle! His situation wasn't good, and the doctors explained to the family that he was a very severe case. But God had heard the prayers of His people. The people responded. The people prayed. The people fasted, and God answered! Today my friend's husband is alive and no longer in the hospital. That's the power of corporate faith, my friends. Miracles can happen—all because of faith!

IT ALLOWS US TO EXPERIENCE THE POWER OF GOD

When God's people express faith together, they experience the power of God in a mighty way. In the book of Acts, the disciples were told to wait for the Holy Spirit to come and fill them. Jesus Christ, the Son of Man, had come to Earth, died for the sins of the world, and been resurrected. He promised His disciples that great power was on the way—the Holy Spirit.

> When the Day of Pentecost had fully come, they were all with one accord in one place. And suddenly there came a sound from heaven, as of a rushing mighty wind, and it filled the whole house where they were sitting. Then there appeared to them divided tongues, as of fire, and one sat upon each of them. And they were all filled with the Holy Spirit and began to speak with other tongues, as the Spirit gave them utterance. (Acts 2:1–4, NKJV)

Before the Holy Spirit came and filled them, the Bible says that they were all in one accord in one place. What does that mean? It means there was agreement among them. They were in harmony with each other. There was a spirit of unity, and because of this, God's power was present.

When there is no agreement among God's people, we lose power. Do we long to see God's power in our lives? I believe we do. I know I do.

Our church family wanted to support our youth attending the Nazarene Youth Conference. This is a big youth conference our denomination prays and plans for every four years. For each youth to attend, it was going to cost $1,500. As a church, we wanted to raise $1,000 per young person. There was no guarantee we could do it, but we decided by faith to do our best and see what happened.

One year in advance, we prayed about raising the funds. The youth operated the fundraiser events, and the church donated its time, talents, and money toward this cause. Due to the commitment of our people and youth to believe, agree, and invest, our church was able to send five teens to the Nazarene Youth Conference. Our district sent a total of twenty-three teens to the conference, and many of them shared how the conference affected them in a powerful way. That's what corporate faith looks like—we believe together, agree, and get to experience God's power!

IT GETS THINGS DONE

When God's people believe together, things get done: reaching a financial goal, sending people on a mission trip, building a home, or sending medical supplies to a country in need. There's no stopping what can happen when we work together and have faith!

A great example of this truth is found in Nehemiah. He was called by God to go back to his homeland and work with the Jews to rebuild the city walls. The walls of Jerusalem had been in ruin since the downfall of Israel. The Bible says that the king of his time allowed Nehemiah to go back and work on the walls.

When Nehemiah got to the city, he could see that there was a lot of work to be done, so he mustered up others to join him on this quest to rebuild the walls.

As they worked, they faced massive discouragement. Some men didn't want to see the Jews succeed. Day after day, despite opposition, pressure, and discouragement, they kept on working and finally they completed the wall: *"So the wall was completed on the twenty-fifth of Elul, in fifty-two days"* (Nehemiah 6:15). Why were the walls completed? Because they'd worked together. They had a spirit of unity. That's what happens when there's corporate faith. What would happen if we agreed in faith?

When I was a young person in my early twenties, the church I was attending began to talk about purchasing land and building a new place of worship. I sat in sermons listening to my pastor talk about the possibility. He preached about the building of the temple of God in Solomon's day. King David had wanted to build it, but his son did instead. As a church, if we were going to see our vision come to pass, we'd all need to believe and give together.

Our pastor challenged us to pray and think about giving above our tithes and regular offering. I'm happy to tell you that I gave during the first three years of the project. Then we pledged again for the next three years. Then we pledged again for the next three years. I was able to contribute for over ten years.

Being part of a project like that helped me see that giving to God is never a waste of time, because I learned to manage my money, give generously, and experience tremendous blessings. I also learned that because we worked on this project together as a church, we got to witness the hand of God move in a mighty way. The church building was completed, and today that church is mortgage-free.

Corporate faith is an unstoppable force when exercised. When we have faith together, we experience powerful unity, miracles, and productivity.

Eight

PERSEVERING FAITH

WHEN I TRAVELLED to Egypt, one of our excursions was to climb Mount Sinai. I was so excited because I wanted to experience the mountain where Moses received the Ten Commandments from God.

When we got to our hotels that night, we were asked to wake up early the next morning. We'd be doing a two-hour climb by camel to get halfway up the mountain. Then we'd travel by foot for another two hours to get to the top of the mountain.

The alarm went off early the next morning, and I got dressed and ready to climb. We completed the camel ride and began to hike by foot in the dark. It was scary and exciting at the same time, but each step brought us closer to the top. But before you get to the very top, there is a section you need to pass, where you can choose to stop or continue. If you stop there, you won't get to the top of the mountain, but even to get that section took perseverance and strength. The tour guide told us that for those who wanted to get to the top, we'd need to keep going. I remember saying to myself, "I am going to the top." Truth be told, getting to the top was more of a psychological challenge than a physical one. But I'm happy to tell you that I got to the top. I saw the sunrise in the morning and the unveiling of the mountains. It was incredible!

Sometimes faith in God is like climbing a mountain. When life is good, our faith is alive and we're walking in confidence. But on those days when we want to give up, we feel like stopping. But just like I had to push myself to get to the top of the mountain, we need to push ourselves in our faith in God.

This is what persevering faith means. You want to give up, but you won't. You keep on believing. You don't pack your bag and stop. You aren't swayed by anyone or anything. You keep your focus. You keep your mind fixed on Jesus and God's Word. People who practise this kind of faith say, "I don't like what I see in my life, but I'm going to keep going." Let's turn to the Bible to learn more about what persevering faith can look like in our lives.

FAITH REFUSES TO ACCEPT NO FOR AN ANSWER

In 2 Kings, we read the story of a well-to-do Shunammite woman who owned a house and was very hospitable. Whenever the prophet Elisha would come into town, she would host him.

One day Elisha told his servant, Gehazi, to call for the Shunammite woman and ask if there was anything they could do for her in gratitude for her kindness (2 Kings 4:13). The woman said she didn't need anything, but Gehazi told Elisha that she had no son and her husband was old. Elisha then asked for the Shunammite woman and told her that within a year, she would hold a son in her arms.

At first, the Shunammite woman refused to accept the word from God, but she did become pregnant and have a son.

The child grew, and one day he said to his father, "My head! My head!" (2 Kings 4:19a). Something wasn't right. The boy sat on his mother's lap, and at noon he died. The mother put her son's body on the bed in Elisha's room.

Most people would accept the death of a loved one. However, in this story, we see a woman deeply convicted that this couldn't be her son's last day. She asked her servant to get her cloak and her donkey, as she was going to see the man of God, Elisha.

As she was getting closer to where Elisha was, Gehazi saw her and ran to her. He asked if everything was all right with her husband and son. Oddly, she replied that she was fine. But when she got to Elisha, she took hold of his feet and said to him, *"Did I ask you for a son, my lord? ... Didn't I tell you, 'Don't raise my hopes'?"* (2 Kings 4:28).

Elisha instructed Gehazi to take his staff and lay it on the boy. However, the woman refused to let Elisha stay put. *"'As surely as the Lord lives and as you live, I will not leave you.' So he got up and followed her"* (2 Kings 4:30).

Gehazi went to the child, but he didn't respond. Finally, Elisha arrived and shut the door. He lay on top of the boy until he felt his body get warm. He got up and then lay on the child again. The boy sneezed seven times and opened his eyes. Elisha called Gehazi to find the Shunammite woman. When she came, he said, *"Take your son"* (2 Kings 4:36b). She fell at his feet and then took her son and went out.

This is an interesting story. The Shunammite woman was barren, but Elisha gave her a word that she would have a son. Then the son dies, and the woman goes back to Elisha. The way in which this child comes back to life will make some people scratch their heads, but I want to focus on the faith of this mother.

The mother witnessed the death of her son in her lap, but something inside of her told her it wasn't over. That's why she went back to Elisha. Even when she saw him, she had to be persistent with him. Then he came and the miracle happened.

We don't understand why her son died or why Gehazi couldn't help. We don't know why Elisha's prayer brought the miracle, but what we do see is that persistence—particularly persistent faith—is powerful.

At some point in my ministry, God called me to another location to serve. After praying about it, I decided to accept the invitation. One of the challenges I faced at the new church was our parking lot situation. The new church building was a heritage site, which meant that our parking lot was across the street and not attached to the church. The church building was also in a very busy tourist area. Hundreds of people travelled to our location just to walk down the street and enjoy the history.

All of that was nice—except on Sunday morning. Despite a sign that read "Property of the church," people didn't seem to realize that the parking lot belonged to us. Every Sunday, cars would drive in as if it were open to the public. As I looked into the problem, I realized that our signage was too long-winded and wordy, which likely caused people to ignore it. By the time I'd arrive on Sunday mornings, about half the lot—roughly ten out of twenty spaces—was already full.

I contacted the city to change our signage, as we had an agreement that the community could use our parking lot for free during the week, and the city would take care of our snow removal and overall lot maintenance.

The city responded with, "Well, it's your parking lot, so you can change the signs if you want." I was upset at this. They were using the parking lot for 90 per cent of the week, so I thought they could change the sign as a gesture of good will. I didn't write that in the email to them, but that's how I felt.

I was very upset and angry, but I decided to take my feelings and the issue to God in prayer. That night, I prayed, "Lord, help them to see the need to change the parking lot signs."

The next day, someone from the heritage department sent me an email that said, "Well, the contract says that if the signs need to be changed, the city will change them."

My heart raced with excitement. Great! Our parking lot signs would be changed!

But he also wrote in the same email: "But I don't think it's necessary to change."

What? Now I was upset again! After calming myself down and taking a few deep breaths, I wrote an email asking him to visit the site on Sunday to see what was going on in the parking lot. He said he would come during the week. The mere fact that he would come by during the week made me happy.

Two men came to the site on a Thursday morning. I explained to them that I didn't want to change our contract with the city, but I did want new signs. I explained that even if it helped reduce the traffic in the lot by 20 to 30 per cent, that would be helpful. The city had been using the lot for fourteen years at no cost. They agreed and said it would be fine.

I was extremely happy with their response. But just like the Shunammite woman who didn't stop until she got a breakthrough, my victory didn't come without faith in God and perseverance. Many times, I had to write back, pray to God, respond and plead my case with the city. But I'm happy to tell you that the new signs have helped us tremendously.

In your walk with God, there will be times when you feel like it's over. Your dream, your hopes, maybe even your desires have come to a closed door. But as you practise persistent faith, you will get an answer, and it can change the outcome of your situation.

FAITH LEAVES NO OTHER OPTION
Persistent faith means you go back to God because no one else can help you and you have no other option. In Matthew 15, Jesus

is passing through Tyre and Sidon and encounters a Canaanite (pagan non-Jew) woman. When she sees Jesus, she cries out to Him for mercy. She explains to Jesus that her daughter is suffering from demon possession.

At first Jesus says, "I was sent only to the lost sheep of Israel" (Matthew 15:24), meaning that He'd been sent to bring salvation to the Jews, but she was a Gentile. A Gentile is someone who is not a Jew.

The disciples try to get Jesus away from her, but she doesn't give up! She approaches Jesus a second time: *"The woman came and knelt before him. 'Lord, help me!' she said. He replied, 'It is not right to take the children's bread and toss it to the dogs'"* (Matthew 15:25–26). Why would Jesus call her a dog? It appears that He's using a bad word. Jews called Gentiles "dogs" because they were pagan worshippers. In this story, Jesus is in a Gentile area.

In the story, it's clear that this woman is desperate. She needs an answer, a breakthrough, and she doesn't back down. Again, she responds to Jesus, *"'Yes it is, Lord,' she said. 'Even the dogs eat the crumbs that fall from their master's table'"* (Matthew 15:27). She decides to use the same language as Jesus, saying that even dogs eat the crumbs from the master's table.

Jesus answers, *"Woman, you have great faith! Your request is granted"* (Matthew 15:28b). Her daughter is healed from that very hour.

Wow! What a story! Jesus grants this woman her request because of her persistent faith. I wonder sometimes what would happen if we just kept on going back to God. If we kept on saying, "God, I am not backing down on this. I need a breakthrough. I need your help. I need your power. I need you to fix this problem." Maybe God would grant our request because of faith and because we had no other option but Him.

In early 2016, our church failed to file paperwork for the government. As a result, we lost our charity status. We began to take steps to regain our charity status. We sent off the paperwork and the registration money. We received a letter in December 2016 asking us many questions. I worked with our church administrator to sort out the details. However, after sending in our answers, we received a second letter asking for more information. I frequently called the government to finalize the details and work out any communication issues.

Unfortunately, we still didn't regain our charity status, and the person I was working with said that he needed to investigate our charity further. The entire situation didn't make sense. We'd filed the paperwork and sent our money. It should have been easily resolved. But our case dragged on. The government worker was blocking our approval. I recall coming off the phone feeling very discouraged. This entire situation caused me to feel helpless and worried. Would we regain our status? How would we issue our tax receipts?

I decided that I needed to increase my prayer and fasting time with God. I prayed for six weeks and fasted one day a week over the paperwork situation. This was in the spring of 2017. After six weeks, I called again, only to discover that our status hadn't changed! I was so mad and confused. "Lord, I am praying! I am fasting! Why aren't you doing anything?"

In the summer of 2017, the government case worker told me that he would no longer be handling my case. I was mad. Did that mean we had to file with someone else and possibly wait another year and a half for a resolution?

I quickly called my prayer partner to share my bad news, and she said to me, "Tina, you've been praying and fasting. What if this is God's answer? What if God wants you to have another worker on your case to grant your request?" I hadn't thought of that option, but what she said resonated with me.

I called the government to find out my new case worker's name and number. I contacted her and explained my case. She requested some letters and information, and after one month of working with her, she granted our request and issued our charitable status number! My two-year battle was finally over!

Why was the battle over? Because I and others had prayed, fasted, and pleaded with God, and we hadn't given up. We were discouraged, but we kept going back to God. In God's time and His way, we received an answer! Persevering faith means we keep going back to God because we have no other option.

Only God can help us.

FAITH KEEPS PRESSING ON DESPITE PRESSURE

Persevering faith means that even when you're being opposed, you choose to keep going. The easy answer might be to quit, but you don't. The book of Nehemiah records God's calling of Nehemiah, a cupbearer to the king, to return to Jerusalem and rebuild the wall. During this time, the Israelite people were being held in captivity by the Babylonian Empire. The temple of Jerusalem had been destroyed, and the walls of the city were in shambles. But now the people were free to move back to Jerusalem. It was reported to Nehemiah that the walls of Jerusalem were broken down and the gates burned with fire (Nehemiah 1:3). Back in those days, the city walls were critical to offering safety from raids, and they symbolized peace and strength.

After seeking the permission of the king, Nehemiah travelled to Jerusalem and led the Israelite people in the rebuilding of the wall. This was a great task the Lord called him to, but he pushed forward anyway; however, while he was fulfilling the call of God on his life, Nehemiah faced major discouragement. Men like Sanballat and Tobiah didn't like what Nehemiah and the Jews were doing, as they might have perceived that the return of the exiled Jews threatened their security, so they ridiculed them (Nehemiah 4:1). Nehemiah prayed and asked God to help them.

When Sanballat and the men heard that the project was moving forward, they plotted against them (Nehemiah 4:8). Nehemiah prayed again. Finally, Nehemiah's enemies threatened to kill them, saying that they would come to the building site (Nehemiah 4:11). This time, Nehemiah devised a plan to have men stationed at the site with swords to fight them off (Nehemiah 4:13).

What did Nehemiah show every time he and his men faced attack? Persevering faith! Every time he faced opposition, he prayed, planned, and kept doing the work God had called him to do. In our lives, we too will face situations that discourage us. Are we willing to exercise persevering faith? Will we keep pushing through for our marriages, our kids, our health, our work, our family and friends, our church, our community, our finances, and our spiritual walk with God, despite the opposition before us? Will we remain in faith?

Here's the beauty of this story: they got the wall done. If we persevere in faith, we will see great things in our lives. We'll see great marriages, great kids, great success, great churches, great communities, great finances, and a solid relationship with God. We will get to the end and reap the rewards. We'll see a change in our life and our world, all because we chose to have faith and press forward.

FAITH HONOURS GOD NO MATTER WHAT

Persevering faith means that when you're put in a tough situation, you honour God no matter what it costs.

In the Old Testament, Daniel was a wise, smart, godly man, but unfortunately while he was captive in Babylon, a law was decreed that anyone who worshipped another god or human being instead of King Darius would be thrown into the lions' den.

Daniel learned about the decree but decided to go into his room with the windows opened toward Jerusalem and pray three times a day on his knees, giving thanks to God (Daniel 6:10–11). The men who had told King Darius to issue this decree found Daniel praying, so they told the king.

King Darius put Daniel in the lions' den and said, *"May your God, whom you serve continually, rescue you!"* (Daniel 6:16b). The king didn't eat or sleep that night, and he had no entertainment. At dawn, he got up and went to the lions' den. When he came near it, he called out to Daniel, asking if his God had rescued him (Daniel 6:20).

Daniel answered:

> May the king live forever! My God sent his angel, and he shut the mouths of the lions. They have not hurt me, because I was found innocent in his sight. Nor have I ever done any wrong before you, Your Majesty. (Daniel 6:21b–22)

God came through and rescued Daniel! But God didn't have to spare Daniel. At other times in the Bible, men and women of God aren't spared; for example, John was beheaded (Matthew 14:9–11), and James died for his faith, too (Acts 12:2). Even though there was a cost and Daniel was pressured to do what was wrong, he made the right choice to persevere and move forward.

If you're in a situation and need to do the right thing, will you choose to love God despite the pressure? Will you serve God even though it's hard? For Daniel, it could have cost him his life.

For some of us, it might cost us a relationship, a job, or physical suffering. Daniel made a choice to follow God, because, for him, it was worth it. What about you?

Nine

WAVERING FAITH

IN OUR WALK with God, we'd like to say that every day is perfect and we exercise faith perfectly, but the truth is, that's not always the case. There are probably days when we're not sure if God will come through. We doubt God's ability to help us, or something doesn't make sense and we feel lost or confused.

This is what I call "wavering faith"—a period when we believe that God is unable to help or can't be trusted. Maybe at one point we believed that God could do the impossible, but we've changed our minds because something tragic has happened. In some cases, these experiences can even threaten our belief in God.

Maybe right now you're going through a period of wavering faith. Despite your situation, God wants you to have a solid, unwavering faith in Him. We might not realize it, but wavering faith is serious. Let's learn what happens when we lack faith in God.

WAVERING FAITH RESTRICTS THE MIRACULOUS

This might be a harsh statement to make, but sometimes our lack of faith in God means we aren't experiencing miracles in our lives. In Mark 6, Jesus is travelling with His disciples to His hometown. When the Sabbath comes, He begins to teach in the synagogue, and the people are amazed by what He says. But there are also people in His hometown who don't understand why He's able to teach. They wonder where He got such wisdom, as He's just the son of Mary and a carpenter. The Word of God says they were offended. Jesus says to them, *"A prophet is not without honor except in his own town, among his relatives and in his own home"* (Mark 6:4b).

Jesus was explaining why the people wouldn't embrace Him. They didn't want to accept that Jesus was the Son of God. The Messiah. The One they had been waiting for. Rather, they made an excuse, and because of their attitude, *"He could not do any miracles there, except lay his hands on a few sick people and heal them. He was amazed at their lack of faith"* (Mark 6:5–6a).

Ouch! This is sad. Think about it—Jesus only performs a few miracles because of their lack of faith. Similarly, our lack of faith could be why we don't see miracles in our lives. From this account in Mark, we learn that the teachings, miracles, and signs of Jesus weren't enough for the people. In fact, because of what Jesus was doing, they disbelieved. They didn't want to accept that Jesus was the Messiah. This meant that more people remained blind, lame, and deaf because of the unbelief of the people.

Think about your own life. Is it possible that God isn't working in a situation due to wavering faith? Like the people in Jesus's hometown, are you refusing to embrace Him for who He truly is? Jesus wants to see our situations change, but do you believe?

• • •

WHEN WE DON'T BELIEVE, WE LIMIT THE
POWER OF GOD.

• • •

If Jesus walked away from His hometown because of their unbelief and only did a few miracles, I wonder what He does due to our unbelief? Does He say, "Well, they don't believe, so I'll move on to the next village"? In our case, God may be saying, "I'll move on to the next person—who does believe." God wants to work in our lives, but we need to remove our unbelief.

WAVERING FAITH IS THE REAL PROBLEM

Maybe you've been crying out to God about a situation and He has heard your prayers, but you're focused on the symptom and not the root of the problem. What if the real problem is something else? Let me explain.

In Mark 9:14–29, Jesus comes down from the mountain, and the crowd sees Him and runs to meet Him. The disciples are there arguing with some people, and Jesus asks them what they're arguing about. At this point, a father speaks up and says that his son is possessed by a spirit that robs him of his speech. He explains that his son becomes mute and has seizures that cause him to fall to the ground, stiffen up, and then foam at the mouth and grind his teeth.

The father then tells Jesus, *"I asked your disciples to drive out the spirit, but they could not"* (Mark 9:18). The spirit in this story is a demon, which is a fallen angel now on the side of Satan, not God. These are evil spirits that work to lead people away from God. The disciples argue over why they were unable to cast out the demon. This is when Jesus steps in and says *"You unbelieving generation ... how long shall I stay with you? How long shall I put up with you?"* (Mark 9:19a).

Jesus is clearly exasperated by the people's unbelief, but despite this, He doesn't dismiss the disciples; instead, He takes action. They bring the boy to Jesus, but the Lord doesn't talk to the spirit but rather to the father. For Jesus, the challenge isn't the power of the demonic spirit but the lack of faith from the crowd, the disciples, and the father.

Jesus asks the father how long his son has been like this. The father explains that it has been since childhood: *"It has often thrown him into fire or water to kill him. But if you can do anything, take pity on us and help us"* (Mark 9:22). Take notice how the father responds to Jesus by saying, *"if you can do anything."* The father isn't doubting that Jesus can do something, but he's uncertain about what He can do. The father is losing hope because the disciples failed him, and his son has been suffering since childhood.

Jesus replies to the father's uncertainty with, *"Everything is possible for one who believes"* (Mark 9:23b). He wants the father to understand that his faith needs to be present in order to see a miracle.

Can you relate to this father? Maybe the difficult situation you're facing is causing you to lose hope because help has been delayed and you've been dealing with it for a long time. But what if the real issue is your lack of belief?

Jesus said that everything is possible for the person who believes, which means God is more than able to turn your situation around. But He wants your faith to be present. I'm not saying that if you have faith, you'll get everything you want, but faith activates God to go to work, to move, to do what He sees fit. There is power when the miracle worker is present and the person seeking the miracle has faith.

Listen to how the father responds to Jesus: *"I do believe; help me overcome my unbelief!"* (Mark 9:24b). Here the father admits his lack of faith. The demon isn't the problem. It's his unbelief. Just like this father, we might need to quit saying that the "demon" in our life is the problem and realize that it's the unbelief we manifest. For this man, the demon caused his son to be sick. What could the demon represent in your life? Maybe you struggle with an addiction like drinking, gambling, drugs, sex, or eating. Perhaps you were rejected or abused growing up. Maybe your spouse didn't keep their marriage commitment. Maybe you believe that your age, the colour of your skin, or your height is holding you back in life. In the story, the father blamed his problem on the demonic spirit, but the real problem was his unbelief.

Perhaps we need to cry out to Jesus like this father did and say, "God, help me overcome my unbelief." In the end, Jesus does battle with the spirit and commands it to leave and never enter him again. Once the real issue was tackled, the boy was set free from the demonic spirit. What breakthroughs would happen in our lives if we simply believed in God?

WAVERING FAITH IS DOUBT

When we need clarity about what to do in a situation, how can we find it? We can exercise many options: read a book, check the internet, call a friend. Those are good things to do, but the Bible tells us, *"If any of you lacks wisdom, you should ask God, who gives generously to all without finding fault, and it will be given to you"* (James 1:5). God's Word tells us to ask Him for wisdom. Therefore, we can ask for wisdom regarding our work, marriage, kids, health, money, and relationships.

But there's one stipulation. James continues: *"But when you ask, you must believe and not doubt, because the one who doubts is like a wave of the sea, blown and tossed by the wind"* (James 1:6). Ouch! Did you catch what he said? If we ask God for wisdom, we can't doubt. How many of us can confess that there have been times when we've sought the Lord's wisdom but at the same time doubted Him? I'll be the first to admit that I've done this. James says that a doubter is like a wave tossed by the wind. What a strong metaphor for how our doubting hearts look when we approach God with our request.

You might be thinking, *Well, I am a human. Yes, I ask God for help, and sometimes I doubt, but it's no big deal.* Do you know what happens when we don't bring our faith to our requests? James says, *"That person should not expect to receive anything from the Lord. Such a person is double-minded and unstable in all they do"* (James 1:7–8). These are hard verses to accept, but the Bible says that when we ask and then doubt, we shouldn't expect anything from God. This means nothing will change. The shift will not come. Our lives will remain stagnant, like a revolving door that remains shut. We must choose with God. Either we believe or we don't, and this is manifested in our faith in Him.

What situation have you brought before God, and did you bring your faith or did you bring your doubt? James's word is clear: we must believe and have faith. If we don't, we won't receive from God, and no breakthrough will come.

WAVERING FAITH MAY CAUSE DRAWBACKS

Is it possible that because we've manifested a wavering faith in God, we've experienced drawbacks in our lives? A story in the Bible does suggest this possibility.

In Luke 1, a priest named Zechariah and his wife, Elizabeth, are described as righteous people who serve God but carry a deep pain in their lives—they are childless. One day, Zechariah, who was chosen by lot, goes into the temple to burn incense. While he's there, the angel Gabriel stands beside him at the altar. When Zechariah sees Gabriel, he's scared, but the angel tells him not to be afraid.

Gabriel explains to Zechariah that his prayer has been heard and Elizabeth will bear a son. They are to call him John, and he will be a joy and delight to them. The angel also tells Zechariah that his son will have a godly and purposeful role in the work of God.

But Zechariah questions the angel, because he and his wife are older. The angel answers him and says:

> I am Gabriel. I stand in the presence of God, and I have been sent to speak to you and to tell you this good news. And now you will be silent and not able to speak until the day this happens, because you did not believe my words, which will come true at their appointed time. (Luke 1:19–20)

Meanwhile, the people outside of the temple are waiting for Zechariah, because he's taking longer than expected. When he finally comes out, they realize that he can't speak and conclude that he's seen a vision, because he keeps making signs.

Why did Zechariah become silent? Because he didn't believe. Wow! When I read this story, I feel sorry for Zechariah, because in his humanity he questioned the angel. But perhaps God expected more from him because he was a priest and follower of God. We may never know why God was so harsh with him but not with Mary, the mother of Jesus, when she asked the angel how she would conceive. Two different situations and people, and both asked a question. One was answered, and the other experienced a drawback. Perhaps God responded based on Zechariah's faith. Zechariah doubted, but Mary had faith.

We learn from this story that when God tells us something, we need to believe Him and not waver. We must have peace with God and let Him have His way in our lives.

Perhaps like Zechariah, we've experienced a drawback because we simply didn't believe. In this story, God silenced Zechariah's mouth. Maybe God has silenced a shift, a situation, or a breakthrough because we didn't believe Him. It might be hard to know the full extent of our disbelief in God, but we learn from this story that it's crucial to take God's word seriously and believe.

BELIEVE AGAIN

We know that God doesn't want our faith to waver but to be strong in all areas of our lives. But if we do doubt God, is it the end of the road between us and the Lord? The answer is no. In John 20, God gives the disciple Thomas a second chance to believe. The story takes place after Jesus has been crucified on the cross (John 19:30) and was laid in the tomb (John 19:42).

In John 20, Christ rises from the dead on the third day and appears to Mary Magdalene. Then Jesus appears to the disciples behind closed doors. The disciples who see Jesus are overjoyed. But Thomas (Didymus) isn't there. The other disciples go and tell him the news about seeing Jesus, but their witness isn't good enough. Rather than believe them, Thomas doubts and says, *"Unless I see the nail marks in his hands and put my finger where the nails were, and put my hand into his side, I will not believe"* (John 20:25). Thomas needed to see it to believe it. In essence, he had a doubting spirit. But that doesn't stop Jesus.

A week later, Jesus shows up and comes through the doors and says to the disciples *"Peace be with you"* (John 20:26b). Then Jesus turns to Thomas and says, *"Put your finger here; see my hands. Reach out your hand and put it into my side. Stop doubting and believe"* (John 20:27b).

Thomas had made three particular requests before seeing Jesus, and Jesus fulfils each one. He asks to see the nail marks, to place his finger where the nails were, and to put his hands into the Lord's side. Jesus met every request, which enabled Thomas to overcome his doubt about Christ and His resurrection.

Just like Thomas, you might have doubted or stopped believing in God. Jesus wants to give you a second chance to believe, and if it's God's will, He can answer your questions. This happened to Thomas. He didn't believe the other disciples, but when Christ revealed Himself, Thomas believed! Maybe we think like Thomas: *I need to see it to believe it.* But what does Jesus say about people who choose to believe and have not seen? *"Then Jesus told him, 'Because you have seen me, you have believed; blessed are those who have not seen and yet have believed'"* (John 20:29).

Who is Jesus talking about when He says *"those who have not seen and yet have believed"*? He's talking about us! We're the people who haven't seen Jesus, yet believe, and He says we are *blessed*. I don't know about you, but that makes me excited. I want to be blessed! May we simply believe in God and remove our wavering faith.

Ten

FAITH AND WAITING

I DON'T LIKE waiting. I don't like to wait for responses to emails. I don't like to wait in line at the store. I don't like to wait for the server at the restaurant. I like it when things happen in my life fast and now. This has been one of my challenges, and when I apply this spirit of impatience to my walk with God, it causes me frustration. I've had to learn the hard way that waiting is spiritual, and it's something I have to do no matter how much I pray, kick, or scream. I've also had to learn to wait with faith.

This was the case for many people in the Bible, such as Abraham and Sarah, Noah, Joseph, and David in the Old Testament. The journey wasn't easy for them. Some had to wait in faith for weeks, months, and even years. As you think about God's promises for your life, consider how you should wait. How can you pass the time with a posture of expectation? Let's take a look at some people in the Bible who had faith and see how they waited.

BE YOUR BEST FOR GOD

As you wait on God and exercise faith, be your best for Him. Joseph is a good example of someone who gave his best to God while he waited in faith.

Before Joseph's life took a downturn, God revealed to him in a dream that he would one day be in power. Joseph tried to share this revelation with his brothers and his father, but they didn't take the information well. His father, Jacob, actually rebuked him (Genesis 37).

The brothers didn't like Joseph because he was their father's favourite. Jacob made a coat of many colours and gave it to Joseph, but he didn't do the same for the other brothers. Due to this favouritism, the brothers mistreated Joseph. They stripped him of his robe and then put him in a cistern. Eventually, they sold Joseph to the Ishmaelites, who in turn sold him to Potiphar.

You can imagine the pain Joseph was feeling at this point in his life. *My brothers hate me. They sold me. I'm never going to see my father again. God, why am I a slave? You gave me a dream to be something more!* All of these thoughts might have run through his head when he considered his life and God's plan.

Despite the pitfalls in Joseph's life, he decided that while waiting on God's plan, he would be his best. The Bible says that he worked for Potiphar, and God gave him success (Genesis 39:2–3). However, Potiphar's wife lusted after Joseph and tried to pursue him, but he consistently refused her. Potiphar's wife then accused Joseph of rape, and he was put in prison. This was another blow to Joseph's life, but the Bible says that while he was in prison, *"the Lord was with him; he showed him kindness and granted him favor in the eyes of the prison warden"* (Genesis 39:21).

No matter what situation Joseph faced, he always put his best foot forward. He kept his head up and persevered. He was consistent and didn't let the circumstances determine his attitude but rather remained steadfast in his faith in God, who granted him success and favour with those around him.

While in prison, Joseph helped two other men, a cupbearer and a baker, who'd had dreams but didn't understand them.

Joseph had the gift of dream interpretation, and he explained that the baker would be executed and the cupbearer would be restored in the palace. Both interpretations were correct. Joseph had asked the cupbearer to remember him when he was restored, but he did not (Genesis 40). Again, Joseph didn't let this setback put a stop to his life. He continued to be his best self. Then, at the right time—God's time—Joseph's life changed.

Two years later, Pharaoh, the most important person in Egypt, was having dreams but nobody could interpret them. Then the cupbearer remembered Joseph and told the palace to retrieve him so that he could interpret Pharaoh's dream. Joseph was able to interpret Pharaoh's dream, and because he was the only one who could do so, he was promoted. Pharaoh gave him a new robe and a ring and made him second in command. He also gave Joseph a wife (Genesis 41). Joseph's life did a full turn. God blessed him, and the promise God had put in his heart came true!

As you wait on God to bless you and bring about His promises, remember to stay faithful to Him and be your best you.

• • •

EVEN THOUGH YOU MIGHT BE IN A
DIFFICULT PLACE, CONTINUE IN FAITH.

• • •

Be consistent. Be faithful to God. Still pray. Still worship. Still give to God. Still serve. Still love God. Then in due time, God can turn your situation around, just as He did for Joseph.

We know that Joseph's life changed, because when he named his first son Manasseh, he said, *"It is because God has made me forget all my trouble and all my father's household"* (Genesis 41:51b). Isn't that wonderful? The name "Manasseh" means forget. Joseph no longer remembered his pain, because God had brought so much joy! If God can do that for Joseph, He can surely do that for us.

PASS YOUR CHARACTER TESTS

While we wait on God, our character will be tested. When faced with doing what's right or wrong, will we choose to do what's right? Our flesh (sinful nature) may want to lead us to fail, but faith and waiting on God means we need to keep our focus and do what's right.

David, a young man after God's heart, was anointed to be the next king of Israel (1 Samuel 16), but King Saul was already in that position. King Saul began disobeying God in his actions. He didn't repent but rather let his pride lead him. God rejected Saul as king and moved on to David. However, the road to the throne was a journey. David didn't become a king overnight.

In 1 Samuel 17, David has reached a high point in his life. He's the only young man brave enough to fight Goliath, a Philistine, who's trying to overtake Israel. David takes his slingshot and stones and, with confidence in God, overcomes the giant Goliath.

The Israelites are impressed by David's courage and fighting ability. They begin to compare him to Saul, saying that Saul has killed thousands, but David has killed tens of thousands. David's fame becomes a problem for Saul, who becomes jealous of David and wants him dead. David and his supporters have to run from Saul.

At one point while being chased, David finds himself in the same cave as Saul and his men. This is his opportunity to kill Saul. One of his men, Abishai, encourages him to do this, but the Bible tells us that David rebuked Abishai.

> "Don't destroy him! Who can lay a hand on the Lord's anointed and be guiltless? As surely as the

Lord lives," he said, "the Lord himself will strike him, or his time will come and he will die, or he will go into battle and perish. But the Lord forbid that I should lay a hand on the Lord's anointed. Now get the spear and water jug that are near his head, and let's go" (1 Samuel 26:9–11)

David was a man of integrity who did not touch Saul, even though he had a right to destroy him. David demonstrated self-control by not trying to make the promise of God happen sooner than its time. He was a patient man of faith and fit to be a king. Eventually, David was crowned King of Israel at the age of thirty.

What about you? When you go through a situation in which you're faced with doing what's wrong or right, how do you respond? If you exercise faith and wait for God to keep His word in your life, then you'll pass your test. It's important that we look at what's going on in our lives right now to determine how we can be obedient to God while we wait.

Many times, we'll be tempted to cut corners and make God's promise happen before it's time. How do we do this? We can rush to get married or have children. We can rush into a job or an investment. We can push to have our own way. But faith and patience in God means you trust His timing. You trust God's Word. You trust that God will do what He says He will do. You understand that God sees the big picture, and that's good enough for you. David passed his character test. What about you?

BE PATIENT

As we wait on God's promises, we have to learn to be patient. This means learning to maintain our peace, even when nothing is moving in our lives. Patience is one of the hardest things for me to exercise, because I'm the kind of person who sees something, works hard, and gets results. But I've learned in my walk with God that I must be patient.

Abraham was a man of faith. Everything in his life was good, except that his wife, Sarah, was barren. They didn't have any children, but God promised Abraham that Sarah would bear him a son (Genesis 15). When God made this promise, Abraham was seventy-five years old. When Abraham was ninety-nine, God told him that in one year, he and Sarah would have a son. When Abraham was one hundred years old, Sarah and Abraham had a son whom they named Isaac.

Think about this story for a moment. When God told Abraham that he would have a son, Abraham was old. Yet the Bible says that Abraham didn't doubt God. In Romans 4, the apostle tells us that against all hope, Abraham believed. Abraham's faith didn't weaken, even though his and his wife's bodies were as good as dead: *"Yet he did not waver through unbelief regarding the promise of God, but was strengthened in his faith and gave glory to God, being fully persuaded that God had the power to do what he had promised"* (Romans 4:20–21).

Abraham believed by faith that God would do what He'd said, no matter his circumstances. But look at the timeline. Abraham was seventy-five years old when he received the promise, but the promise wasn't fulfilled until he was one hundred years old. We don't know why the promise took so long. Perhaps it was delayed because Abraham and Sarah tried to "help" God when Abraham was eighty-six years old. At that time, Sarah told Abraham to have a baby with their servant Hagar, and they had a child named Ishmael (Genesis 16). But Ishmael was not the promised child. Isaac was, and he finally came when Abraham was one hundred years old (Genesis 21).

I've always wondered why it took so long for the promise to come to pass. I don't have an answer, because I'm not God. But what has struck a chord with me is that Abraham continued to believe, and he believed with patience: *"And so after waiting patiently, Abraham received what was promised"* (Hebrews 6:15). This attitude of patience is pertinent to our lives as well. If we want to see a breakthrough with God's promises, we'll have to wait.

We must understand that sometimes what God has put in our hearts won't happen overnight. It could be days, weeks, months, or even years. No matter what you're waiting for, are you willing to be patient?

JOY IS COMING. GET READY!
Waiting on God has an expiry date. You won't be waiting forever, and when the promises come to pass, you can anticipate joy.

In Luke 2 after Jesus was born, Mary and Joseph took Him to the temple to be presented to the Lord. The Bible says there was a man there named Simeon. Simeon was righteous and devout, and he was waiting for the consolation of Israel. The Holy Spirit was on him (Luke 2:25). God had revealed to Simeon by the Holy Spirit that he would see the Messiah before he died.

That day, the Holy Spirit told Simeon to go to the temple courts. When Simeon saw Jesus, he took Him in his arms and praised God, saying, *"Sovereign Lord, as you have promised, you may now dismiss your servant in peace. For my eyes have seen your salvation"* (Luke 2:29–30).

What a moment that was for Simeon! Think about this with me. God tells you something. You wait, and now it happens! I'm sure many of us have gone through the emotional and mental roller coaster of asking "Did I hear God correctly?" or "Maybe this is all in my head." Yet God's promise to Simeon became reality in his life!

My friends, as you read this story, may you anticipate joy! When the loved one you have been praying for comes to Jesus, when the sick person you love is healed, when God puts aside a job for you, when you get married, when you have that child, when peace comes to your country, and when the ministry God has put in your heart comes to pass, be like Simeon and praise God too! The days were long. The cries to God were real. But when everything is said and done, and it's time, the very things God spoke into your life will come, and you won't remember the pain of waiting or the suffering anymore. All you will have is unspeakable joy!

Eleven

MODELLING FAITH

I'M A VISUAL learner. When I can see how to do something, I'm able to do it. But if I have to do something by following written instructions, it will take me longer. Usually I get frustrated with the process when I don't finish quickly enough. That's why I like to go online and Google what I need to learn. I'll watch a video that shows me step-by-step what to do and how to do it. I can also pause the video at any point to ensure I'm on the right track.

In our Christian walk, we can look to people as "models" of faith. It's like watching a video. I'm not talking about the models you see on TV but about someone who shows you how to be like Jesus by being loving, kind, and giving through their actions and words. When you have a Christian model in your life to show you how to practise your faith daily, it will be easier for you to be faithful too. He or she serves to inspire and encourage you. Let's consider the different ways in which our faith can be modelled for us.

GENERATIONAL MODELLING

Faith can be powerfully passed on through generationally modelling. Paul, a man of faith, wrote a letter to Timothy, who had become near and dear to his heart. Paul said to him, *"I am reminded of your sincere faith, which first lived in your grandmother Lois and in your mother Eunice and, I am persuaded, now lives in you also"* (2 Timothy 1:5). In this portion of the letter, Paul mentions Timothy's family line of faith. His grandmother Lois loved God, and so did his mother, Eunice. Paul was persuaded that the same fire and faith lived in Timothy!

Sometimes we underestimate the power of modelling our faith as grandparents and parents. We don't see the blessings, but modelling faith can be passed down and be deeply rooted in the generations to come. My grandfather on my mother's side of the family was exposed to a Lutheran church, and through that interaction, made a decision to be a follower of Christ.

Growing up, though, I never saw him go to church and read the Bible, but he was a gentle and quiet man. His faith in Jesus Christ did have an impact on him. When my grandmother was pregnant with my mother, my grandfather wanted his new child to have a Christian name, so my mother's name is Mary. She was born on April 10, 1959, in Guyana.

Fast-forward to 1975. My mother was married to my father, and they immigrated to Toronto, Canada, to start a new life. They worked hard and built a life with their five daughters. When I was about eight years old, a lady from the community knocked on our door and invited my mother to Emmanuel Church of the Nazarene. My mother took the invitation seriously and began to attend services there. Eventually, my sisters, my father, and I decided to follow Jesus Christ, too. At the tender age of eight, I gave my heart to Jesus.

Looking back now, I can see the power of generational Christian modelling. My grandfather's choice to follow Jesus inspired my mother. My mother's choice to be a committed follower of

Christ inspired me. We began to attend worship services regularly when I was eight years old, and I've been attending worship services to this day. When I was nineteen years old, I felt a call to serve God in a more specific way, and I made a choice to take that call more seriously when I was in my early twenties. Now I'm a pastor serving in the Church of the Nazarene.

To all the grandparents and parents who are faithfully serving God and doing their best to encourage their grandkids and children to be followers of Jesus Christ: do not stop what you're doing. You are impacting your grandchildren and kids. You may or may not witness the fruit you're producing in them in this lifetime, but keep praying, fasting, serving, giving to God, and attending worship services. Keep on spiritually investing, because your modelling is noticed. Timothy was who he was because of his grandmother and his mother. I am who I am today because of my grandfather and my mother.

MODELLING THROUGH IMITATION

Another way of modelling faith in our lives comes through imitation. A great example of this is the apostle Paul. In one of his letters to the Christian community in Corinth, he writes, *"Follow my example, as I follow the example of Christ"* (1 Corinthians 11:1). At first glance, this sounds a little conceited. But on the contrary, Paul wanted the churches to follow his lead as he followed Christ. Essentially, he was saying, "You look at me as I look to Christ to overcome temptations, trials, and challenges in order to live a holy and pleasing life for God." This verse reminds us that God uses people in our lives as examples of Christ so that we understand how to live out our Christian walk with God.

I can name people in my life who have been amazing Christian models and whom I want to emulate. For example, my very first pastor embodied what it means to be Christ-like. The characteristic that stands out for me is gentleness. He spoke and carried himself with gentleness and love.

Another pastor in my life has the gift of giving. He'll give up his time, energy, and money just so that someone else feels joy and happiness. Over the years, he has extended that spirit of giving to me and my family.

Another colleague and friend of mine has the gifts of mercy and compassion through hospitality; I want to imitate her love for others through the generous gift of food, fellowship, and home. She's happy to have you come over, and she'll make you something so that you feel the love of Christ.

Another colleague and friend of mine has a passion for prayer and worship. She prays, prays, and prays. She sings, sings, and sings to God. She'll pray for others and raise her hands and worship God no matter what season she's in. She's a powerhouse, and she embodies the spirit of perseverance.

My friend and colleague from school has travelled the world to preach the gospel and donate food, clothes, and supplies. She has such a heart for people. Her gifts are evangelism and teaching the Word. She'll do anything for someone to hear the gospel message.

Finally, my good friend has the gift of compassion. She has a big heart and is empathetic to you and your situation. She knows how to listen and give a compassionate answer. People like her are hard to find.

These are the individuals in my life whom I want to imitate so that I become more like Jesus.

BIBLE MODELS
Some people have made an impact on my life, but I've never met them. I call these people "Bible models." These are men and

women who have modelled for us what faith looks like and how to walk it out.

One model is Abraham. God called Abraham to leave his country, his father, and his family, and he didn't hesitate to do what God asked him to do, *"So Abram went, as the Lord had told him"* (Genesis 12:4a).

Then God told Abraham he would have a son, even though he and his wife, Sarah, were older. The Bible says, *"Abram believed the Lord, and he credited it to him as righteousness"* (Genesis 15:6). After Abraham received his son, God called him to sacrifice the boy. This call was probably a crisis moment in Abraham's life. He'd believed that God would grant him a son, and now he was being asked to sacrifice him. He had to choose whether to obey God. Abraham chose to trust in God and was ready to do His will. Thankfully, God stopped him and told him not to touch the boy. Abraham models for us what it looks like to listen to God.

Another person in the Bible who shows us the same kind of faith is Mary. Mary was a simple girl who lived in Nazareth, and God called her to be the mother of Jesus. The Old Testament prophets had said that a virgin would bear a child, and she was the one God chose to fulfill this task!

When the angel Gabriel came to her, he explained that she was favoured. The angel told her that she would bear a son, and He was to be named Jesus. He would save His people from their sins. Mary didn't understand how she could have a son, but the angel explained that she would conceive by the Holy Spirit. Mary agreed to what the angel said and showed us what it means to have faith.

Maybe you don't have people in your life who can model faith for you, but we have people in the Bible, like Abraham and Mary, who show us what it looks like. We can also look to Noah, who built the ark; Enoch, who walked with God; Joseph, who was faithful even in jail; Deborah, who led the Israelites; Esther, who was brave and went to the king; Peter and Paul, who preached the gospel; and the disciples, who followed Jesus. When in doubt, we can always circle back to the Bible to find men and women of faith.

PARENTS AS MODELS

It's one thing to tell your kids to love God, but to live it out and do what God calls you to do sends a strong message to children. In Deuteronomy 6, God tells parents to model faith to their children and to impress God's commandments on their hearts (Deuteronomy 6:7).

How does that look today? Whether you're at home, going for a walk, or driving somewhere, tell your kids about God! Children gain more from seeing what their parents do with their faith than by just going to church or a Sunday school class. Seeing your faith in action speaks more powerfully to them than what they read or hear.

I remember my mother taking us kids on the bus to go to church, no matter what the weather was like. Her determination to be in the church taught me to persevere in my walk with God. My mother would spend her nights reading her Bible. I can recall getting up at night and seeing her with her Bible, which left a big impression on me and even now reminds me of the hard work of studying the Word.

My father liked to pray over all his daughters on Sunday mornings, which today reminds me of the power of prayer. He would lay hands on us and ask God to protect and take care of us. He'd also give people money or food, demonstrating the gift of mercy and compassion.

When parents obey the Word of God and live it out, they provide a physical reality for children to refer to in times of trouble. When faced with the same situation later in life, children can say,

"I remember the time my mother prayed" or "the time my father went to the hospital to visit someone." This kind of modelling of faith is the duty and call of all parents.

As we can see, modelling is key to faith in God. It helps us to see what faith looks like in real people dealing with real situations. Whom do you want to imitate, and who do you want imitating you?

Twelve

FAITH AND OBEDIENCE

I ONCE HEARD a pastor on the radio say that the Christian walk with God is characterized by two things: faith and obedience. As I continued listening, I pondered this statement in my heart and mind, silently agreeing with the pastor. Truly, God is calling us to always obey Him, and this is coupled with faith. This simply means that we do what God asks of us because we want to do what is right and follow God's will. In our day-to-day walk with God, what does that look like? The Bible gives us insight into what faith and obedience look like.

TAKING GOD AT HIS WORD

Exercising faith and obedience means that when God tells us to do something, we trust His Word and do what He says. In John 5, Jesus was in Jerusalem near the Sheep Gate at a pool. In those days, many disabled people would lie at the pool, hoping to be healed. Some were blind, and others, lame or paralyzed.

One man, whom John refers to as an *"invalid,"* had been going to the pool for thirty-eight years. When Jesus saw him, He learned that he'd been in this condition for a long time. Jesus asked him if he wanted to get well. The man explained that every time he wanted to get into the pool, no one was there to help him. *"Then Jesus said to him, 'Get up! Pick up your mat and walk.' At once the man was cured; he picked up his mat and walked"* (John 5:8–9).

This is a story about healing and also about faith and obedience. Jesus told him to get up, pick up his mat, and walk. The man could have doubted God, but he didn't. He picked up his mat and walked.

What about us? So much in our lives is dependent on our faith and obedience to God, specifically to His Word. What has God called you to do? Have you been doing it? Or have you been doubting God?

When I was in my mid-twenties, I was in the middle of my Master of Divinity program. Six months before graduating in May 2007, I began to pray about where God was leading me. While I was praying, God was working. The church I was attending had a vision to plant a church thirty minutes away from their location. After holding discussions and spending time in prayer, they proposed that I consider leading the new church.

The senior pastor and another staff member met with me and explained their vision. They said that the church board supported the idea of me becoming the church plant pastor. I was quite shocked that they believed in me, but I was also humbled. The senior pastor explained that if I wanted to become the pastor, I needed to attend an assessment retreat to confirm whether I had the gifts and grace for the position.

Off I flew to Kansas City to be assessed by strangers. I spent three days preaching and planning, with people evaluating my leadership skills. The results were positive, and I was approved to lead the plant. They completed a report for me to give to the church board. But I still wasn't sure if this was the direction God was leading me in. I knew it was a great opportunity, but I didn't have the assurance until after returning from the trip.

While I was driving to an evening service, God began to speak to me. I was listening to a song and then I heard this line: "Lord, to give up, I'd be a fool." For some reason, those words penetrated my heart. I began to speak to God: "Lord, I'm very nervous about opening up this church. What if I fail?"

God reassured me, and I heard, "Tina, you're already giving up and you haven't even tried." My time with God confirmed that He wanted me to step out and be obedient. About a year and a half later, we opened the church, and I never looked back.

TRUSTING GOD WITH THE OUTCOME

Faith and obedience also require that we always give our best and trust God, even though we don't have all the answers. Cain and Abel are great examples of this truth.

Abel kept flocks, while Cain worked the soil (Genesis 4:2). Over some time, Cain brought the fruits of the soil to God as an offering; his brother Abel brought an offering, too—fat portions from some of his firstborn flock. The Bible says that God looked at Abel's offering with favour. Why? Because Abel brought his best to God, whereas Cain brought his leftovers and kept the best for himself. Cain became angry, but God told him not to be downcast and to do what was right (Genesis 4:6). Unfortunately, Cain let his anger and jealousy overtake him, and he murdered Abel.

It's sad that Abel died, but we can learn from how he lived his life. Abel lived a life of faith and obedience to God. He gave his offering to God *first*—and he gave his best. In doing this, he was saying to God, "I don't know how everything else in my life will work out, but I'm trusting you to provide for me as I give my best to you." God was pleased with Abel's offering.

God wants us to give our best to Him, and we do this through faith and obedience, even when we don't know how things will work out. Today we don't give animal offerings, but we can give our lives to God. *"Therefore, I urge you, brothers and sisters, in view of God's mercy, to offer your bodies as a living sacrifice, holy and pleasing to God—this is your true and proper worship"* (Romans 12:1) When Paul says give our bodies, he's talking about our lives. When you think about your life, do you feel that you give your best to God and trust Him to work it out?

We originally had about forty people interested in the church plant, but as we planned, some people backed out of their commitment. In the end, a small group came with us. But despite disappointments and setbacks, I still gave my best to God. I was obedient, and I still preached my sermon as if there were hundreds of people in the room committed to God. I gave my best to God in terms of my time and my gifts. I taught the Word, prayed for people, visited others, and gave counsel. I went around the area weekly to pray for the community. I also gave generously to God in terms of my money, despite feeling that we weren't going in the right direction. I was obedient in faith to God.

Whatever you're going through, God wants you to give your best in faith and obedience, trusting that He'll work it out. As I'm writing this, it has been over seventeen years since we started that plant. I didn't always know how we'd make it, but we did. Whatever season you're in, be the best parent, spouse, worker, and layperson, and give your best to God, trusting Him to work it out.

WHEN FAITH AND OBEDIENCE DEFY LOGIC

God wants us to obey Him in faith even when it defies our logical understanding of the situation. In Joshua 6, Joshua and the Israelites weren't ready to claim the land God had promised them, as they needed to overcome the people at Jericho. God gave them instructions to march around the city once for six days. On the seventh day, they were to march around the city seven times with the priests blowing trumpets. Finally, *"When you hear them sound a long blast on the trumpets, have the whole army give a loud shout; then the wall of the city will collapse and the army will go up, everyone straight in"* (Joshua 6:5).

These seem like very odd instructions, and many questions could be asked. Why walk around the city six times? Why on the seventh day walk around it seven times and then shout? Why not defeat them by going straight into the city? These are good questions, but the Bible says that Joshua obeyed God's command. Here's what's amazing—everything God said came true. That's why the writer to the Hebrews wrote, *"By faith the walls of Jericho fell, after the army had marched around them for seven days"* (Hebrews 11:30).

How did they defeat the city of Jericho? By faith—by simply taking God at His word even though it didn't make sense. Sometimes God asks us to do something that doesn't make sense and defies logic, but we follow through because He said it.

I remember when God started to move in my heart about moving our church to another location. I was serving in one city, but I began to feel that God wanted me to move to another city. But I didn't want to. I'm just being honest. The new location was in a traditional building, and I'd be leaving a contemporary space. I was also concerned about losing congregation members in the process of moving, which did happen when we eventually made the move.

God had asked me to lead a church merger. On the outside, nothing about the move made sense. But out of that move, one key situation arose for me. Earlier, I shared about praying for a woman with sciatica pain who was healed. Over the years, I lost contact with that couple. But one spring day in 2024, I was going to a church down the street from where I now served to attend a local ministerial meeting. When I walked into the church building, a woman saw me and came up to me.

"I know you," she said.

I honestly didn't remember her, so I apologized for that.

"Do you remember Christina and Anthony?" she asked.

At first, I was confused, but then she said, "My husband's name is Anthony."

As soon as she said that, I realized that this was the woman I'd laid hands on over fifteen years earlier. I couldn't believe it! I was shocked and so was she. She then said, "Let's take a picture and send it to my husband." We made plans to keep in touch and had lunch that same summer. I learned that she never had a relapse and was now serving as a pastor down the street where I was serving! How amazing is that?

As I reflected on reconnecting with her, I said to God, "If I hadn't switched ministry locations, I never would have run into Christina. Lord, perhaps you know what you're doing and you had a reason for moving me." Sometimes, what God asks of us won't make sense, but we must be obedient to Him. When we are, He will surprise us in ways we can't even imagine.

GOING AGAINST THE CULTURE

Choosing to follow God can put us in situations where our actions go against the culture. When I say culture, I'm talking about the norms and values of your friends, family, and community. It's hard to go against the culture, but we must follow through with God's plan.

This was the case for Moses's parents. Moses was born during the time that Pharaoh had ordered every Hebrew male baby to be thrown into the Nile (Exodus 1:22). Despite this law, Moses's mother hid him for three months and then put him in a papyrus basket, coated it with tar and pitch, and put him on the bank of the Nile (Exodus 2:3).

Pharaoh's daughter found the baby and felt sorry for him. Moses's sister, Miriam, had been watching and offered to find a Hebrew woman to nurse the baby (Exodus 2:7). Miriam brought back their mother, who was now able to nurse her son. Talk about God working even when the culture is against you! Pharaoh's daughter named him Moses.

Moses became a man in Egypt, but at the age of forty had to flee when he murdered an Egyptian. He then lived in Midian, where he got married. Eventually, God called Moses to go back to Egypt to demand that Pharaoh release the Israelites, who were in severe bondage and slavery to the Egyptians. At the age of eighty, Moses returned to Egypt and was able to prove to them, through a series of plagues, that Yahweh was God. Pharaoh eventually freed the Israelites, and they left Egypt.

Moses lived and was able to do what he did for God because of one act of faith. The Bible says, *"By faith Moses' parents hid him for three months after he was born, because they saw he was no ordinary child, and they were not afraid of the king's edict"* (Hebrews 11:23). If his parents hadn't acted on faith, Moses would have died. Imagine if they had given in to the culture—we might not have the first five books of the Bible or the stories of the Red Sea, water from the rock, and God providing for the Israelites in the desert.

Faith and obedience mean going against the crowd. This will be difficult at times, because culture will push you to think and behave one way, and God's Word calls for us to go in a different direction. But let's stand our ground and continue to do what's right.

I was in a situation once where I needed to decide whether to say something or not. If I didn't say anything, then the person would think that their behaviour was acceptable when it wasn't. If

I did say something, that person would feel offended. After praying and reflecting on the situation, I decided to say something. I confronted the person in love, but they didn't take it well. Even after the conversation, they didn't believe they'd done anything wrong. But here's the key: When we don't stand for what's right, the truth gets lost or muddled. But when we do say something, we plant a seed in the person's heart, and by the power of the Holy Spirit, he or she can change their mind and repent.

Will we win over everyone when we go against the culture? No, but even if our actions impact one person, then it's worth taking the right stand. The person who hears the truth, repents, and moves forward in the right direction will live in surrender and obedience to God, rather than be trapped by Satan's lies. That's why we need to take a stand and say something, even if it's not popular. The Bible reinforces this truth:

> My brothers and sisters, if one of you should wander from the truth and someone should bring that person back, remember this: Whoever turns a sinner from the error of their way will save them from death and cover over a multitude of sins. (James 5:19–20)

Thirteen

FAITH AND TESTING

EXERCISING FAITH IN God won't always be easy. In fact, walking out your faith will sometimes mean making hard decisions. Should I abort my child? Should I walk away from this relationship? Should I lie at work to keep my job? This is what we mean by faith and testing, and when it is tested, what will we choose? Will we follow the crowd, or will we follow God? Despite how hard life gets, good things can come from faith and testing as we stay focused on God.

TESTING DEVELOPS OUR CHARACTER

When our faith is tested, God is doing something bigger in us than what meets the eye. He's developing our character. That's why James wrote this to the church: *"Consider it pure joy, my brothers and sisters, whenever you face trials of many kinds, because you know that the testing of your faith produces perseverance"* (James 1:2). Wait a minute, did James just say that we're to consider it pure joy to go through pain? He sure did! In essence, James is saying that we should look at our trials as a good thing because God is testing our faith to develop perseverance.

You might be thinking, *Well, I don't want to go through a trial.* Listen, nobody does, but we all have to go through something we didn't expect to happen, like losing a loved one or a job, going through a breakup or divorce, dealing with a health challenge or a problem at work. Yet the Bible teaches that without trials, we won't learn how to press on, pray, depend on God, and remain steadfast before Him.

What trial in your life developed perseverance in you? For me, it was during a time when I had to deal with a broken relationship. I spent a lot of time asking God why the relationship ended and why He hadn't protected me. I didn't get full answers, but through the trial, I learned to pray to God and draw closer to Him. Without this trial, my spiritual walk with God wouldn't have shifted. Looking back now, I can say that the trial was a good thing, but while I was going through it, it was a nightmare. At times, we'll all feel this way. We don't like the pain, the hurt, or the anger, but through it, we will see that God loves us and cares about us. He wants the best for us. What was difficult at the time was used by God to make me more like Him.

TESTING TEACHES US TO DO WHAT'S RIGHT

As we walk with God, we will be tempted to do wrong things. When this happens, our faith will be tested. The biblical story of Shadrach, Meshach, and Abednego illustrates this point. All three men decided to do what was right, despite what the world was doing.

During their time, King Nebuchadnezzar set up an idol of himself and ordered all the people to bow down and worship it. Some of the workers saw that these three men didn't bow down and reported them to the king. The king was angry and called for the men. The men responded:

> King Nebuchadnezzar, we do not need to defend ourselves before you in this matter. If we are thrown into the blazing furnace, the God we serve is able to deliver us from it, and he will deliver us from Your Majesty's hand. But even if he does not, we want you to know, Your Majesty, that we will not serve your gods or worship the image of gold you have set up. (Daniel 3:16–18)

Wow! These men were confident that God could save them, and if He didn't, they still weren't going to worship the king! Talk about bold faith—but more importantly, when they were put in the line of fire and tested, they did what was right.

In our walk with God, we will be tested. A friend might want to gossip about someone. They might want you to lie about something at work. Maybe your boyfriend or girlfriend wants to be sexually involved with you. Maybe your family doesn't want you to attend church because they're not Christian. Whatever test we go through, we have to make a choice. Let's be like these men and stand our ground.

When I worked for a corporate office, my job allowed me to interact with customers as I mediated between them and the store. Whenever I conducted calls and carried out my responsibilities, I did my best to be upfront and honest. Often I could have lied to the customer to mislead them or end the situation, but I told the truth.

One day while working on a case, one of my colleagues noticed this and said that she appreciated my honesty with the customer. I told her, "I'm not going to lie to the customer." I made a choice to be honest because that's what the Bible says to do, but I also knew that if I lied to the customer and broke their trust, I'd have a bigger issue. She said that she admired that about me and decided that it would be best for her to be honest, too.

• • •

IN OUR WALK WITH GOD, WE'LL BE PRESSURED TO DO WRONG THINGS, BUT WHEN THIS HAPPENS, OUR FAITH IS BEING TESTED, SO WE MUST DO WHAT'S RIGHT.

• • •

TESTING REVEALS OUR INTEGRITY BEFORE GOD

When our faith is tested, we have to choose how to respond, and our response will reveal our spiritual integrity.

In the Bible, a man named Job was blameless and upright before God. One day Satan was talking to God, and God asked him if he was aware of Job, whom He called *"my servant"* (Job 1:8). Satan knew that Job was blessed, because he referred to the hedge God had placed around him, claiming that was the reason for his faith. He told God that if He struck Job, Job would curse God. God responded to Satan and said, *"Very well, then, everything he has is in your power, but on the man himself do not lay a finger"* (Job 1:12). From that point on, Job's life took a full turn. He lost assets and his family. Nothing good was going his way.

But despite all the pain and sorrow Job experienced, he remained faithful to God. He did not curse God.

> At this, Job got up and tore his robe and shaved his head. Then he fell to the ground in worship and said:
> "Naked I came from my mother's womb,
> and naked I will depart.
> The Lord gave and the Lord has taken away;
> may the name of the Lord be praised."

> In all this, Job did not sin by charging God with wrongdoing. (Job 1:20–22)

Job worshipped God and didn't point his finger at Him! Wow! This is a man whose roots are deep in God. If there was a time when Job could have lashed out at God, that was it, but he didn't.

I'd like to be able to say that when I've faced deep trouble in my life, I've worshipped God and kept my integrity. But unfortunately, my faith hasn't been at the same level as Job's. Perhaps as I grow and mature, I will become as spiritually strong as he was. But when I've faced pain, I've questioned God: Why did this happen to me?

Job has what I call an "even if" faith. No matter what happened, he was still going to worship and trust God. Do you have that kind of faith? Even if you lost your health, your job, your house, your family, or your money, would you worship God? Would you still clap your hands in worship? Would you still say that God is good? Job knelt and worshipped God. What a profound reaction to pain in life.

In this story, Job's pain was caused by Satan. In our walk with God, our struggles might be the work of the enemy. You will still have to decide how to respond. When your faith is being tested, will you trust God? Clearly Job trusted in God. What about you?

TESTING REVEALS TO GOD HOW MUCH WE LOVE HIM

Sometimes God might test our faith to determine what we love more: Him or the promise He gave us. Let me explain. There's a story in the Bible that was always difficult for me to understand as a child. It's the story of Abraham being tested by God.

In Genesis 12, God promises Abraham that he will be a great nation. In Genesis 15, God promises Abraham a son. In Genesis

21, Sarah has the promised child, but then in Genesis 22:1, God tests Abraham.

All this time, Abraham has been faithful, and now God decides to test him. In our walk with God, there will be times when what we're going through is a test. What did God test Abraham with? He told him to sacrifice his son. This makes no sense. God told Abraham he would have a son. God gave him his son, Isaac. Now God asks him to take that same son and sacrifice him. What is going on here? Will Abraham listen to God's voice and obey?

What must have been swirling in his head? *God, you told me I'd have descendants. If I sacrifice my son, won't I lose my promise?* Abraham had to choose between reason or trusting in God. The Bible says, *"Abraham reasoned that God could even raise the dead, and so in a manner of speaking he did receive Isaac back from death"* (Hebrews 11:19).

In the end, Abraham does what God asked him to do, but Isaac isn't sacrificed. Instead, God appears on the scene: *"Now I know that you fear God, because you have not withheld from me your son, your only son"* (Genesis 22:12b). Whew, what a relief! Isaac doesn't have to die, and because of what Abraham did for God, it confirmed that he truly loved the Lord more than any gift given to him.

We learn from this story that God tested Abraham to see if he'd be willing to give up something he loved and the promises of God for his life. Abraham was willing, and this proved to God that he was committed to Him. In life, you too might face a situation like Abraham. God might ask you to do something, or give up something, that contradicts what He told you about your life. Will you give it up? Will you trust God, even though it doesn't make sense? Will you reason that God will somehow make a way, even though there is no way? Abraham trusted God, and it showed God that he loved Him more than anything else. God is calling us to do the same thing.

Fourteen

FAITH AND WITNESS

SOMETIMES WHEN WE exercise faith in God, something more is going on behind the scenes. We can't see it, but our faith serves a bigger picture. We tend to think that everything going on in our lives is about us, and not others. Sometimes it is, but sometimes it's not. We don't always know, but in those times when we're unsure about a situation, our best response is to simply have faith in God and trust that He's doing something for His purposes. In particular, He might be witnessing to us and to those who do not believe in Him.

WITNESSING TO US

• • •

> SOMETIMES TROUBLING LIFE CIRCUMSTANCES HELP US TO SEE THE CHARACTER AND POWER OF GOD.

• • •

In the Bible, the disciples take a boat ride with Jesus. Everything is going well, until a storm comes. This isn't just any storm—it's a dangerous one. But while the storm is raging, Jesus is sleeping in the stern. In a state of fear and confusion, the disciples say to Jesus, *"Teacher, don't you care if we drown?"* (Mark 4:38b).

Just picture the scene. I'm sure we've all seen our share of storms in life when we wondered what was going on. Storms like trying to raise a child, facing pressure at work, dealing with health challenges, navigating marital disagreements, or worrying about the safety of your country. Just like the disciples, we've felt that Jesus has been sleeping. Sleeping when we pray. Sleeping when we cry out to Him. Sleeping when we feel worried, depressed, and anxious. Just like them, we've said to God, "Don't you care?"

Jesus gets up and rebukes the wind. He says, *"Quiet! Be still!"* (Mark 4:39b), and the wind dies down and it's calm. When this happens, the disciples are now afraid not of the storm but of Jesus. Jesus says to them, *"Why are you so afraid? Do you still have no faith?"* (Mark 4:40b). At this point, they realize that Jesus is more than who they thought. They ask each other why even the wind and waves obey Him.

Their terrible situation caused the disciples to look at Jesus differently. Wait a minute—maybe Jesus is more than just a man. Maybe He's a prophet. No, maybe He's a great teacher. Or could He be ... the Son of God? They were still learning, and their faith was still growing. But we know that they learned that day that the wind and waves had to obey Jesus. Faith in this story was all about looking at Jesus and recognizing Him for who He was—God with us!

Sometimes God uses the storms of life to witness to us, to show us that He is bigger than the mountain we see and bigger than the waves and wind. But above all, God is bigger than our marital problems, dysfunctional kids, financial challenges, and health problems. God knows what He's doing, and as we cry out to Him, He will answer and show us His ways.

Sometimes God answers right away, and other times He takes His time, but we can trust that a perfect God knows what He's doing. He's never late but always on time. When God does come through, we have to stand back and be amazed. We need to humble ourselves and praise Him for who He is. He is not limited. He is mighty and all-powerful, and just like the disciples, we'll say, "Who is this?"

WITNESSING TO OTHERS

Sometimes what's going on in our lives serves as a witness to others. In another story, a woman named Rahab, a prostitute, became instrumental in helping two spies from Israel who were scoping the land of Jericho.

These men stayed at Rahab's house, even though she was a prostitute. The king of Jericho learned about the two spies and sent his men to tell Rahab to bring them out. But Rahab had hidden the men on her roof. She lied and told the men that the spies had left.

After the men left, Rahab spoke to the spies and explained that she knew God had given the land to them. She said that the people were in fear because of them, as they'd heard about God drying up the water of the Red Sea, and how they'd destroyed Sihon and Og, two kings of the Amorites east of the Jordan. *"When we heard of it, our hearts melted in fear and everyone's courage failed because of you, for the Lord your God is God in heaven above and on the earth below"* (Joshua 2:11). Rahab requested that when the Israelites came to take the land, they spare her house and her family. The spies agreed and decided to mark her home so that it wouldn't be touched.

One intriguing aspect of this story is that a prostitute helps the Israelites; another is that she tells the spies what's been heard about their God. She was not an Israelite—she was a woman on the outside—but she might as well have been one of them, because she understood what God was doing for the Israelites. God's reputation was spreading—so much so that Rahab called Him the true and living God. The writer of Hebrews confirms Rahab's faith in God: *"By faith the prostitute Rahab, because she welcomed the spies, was not killed with those who were disobedient"* (Hebrews 11:31).

This story tells us that Israel's faith in God—and God's faithfulness to His word—was spreading His name to other nations. It was making the Canaanites think that perhaps there was only one true God and that the Israelites' God was greater than the gods they served.

A couple of years ago, God began to speak to me about my friend and his wife. God had a word of encouragement for them, so I sent them a word telling them to trust God in their situation. I took a risk in sending them this email message, because I didn't know how they'd respond, and they don't share my belief in Jesus Christ. But by faith I sent them the message.

In response, the wife sent me an email that read, "I don't even have words to express what this email means to me." She asked if I'd be able to meet with them.

I made time to meet, and during that meeting, they explained that their issue was getting harder and they weren't finding resolution. It was a time of discouragement. I believe my role was to be an encouragement to them.

Some time passed, and my sister and I got an email from them, sharing their good news. This was a miracle for them, and it all started because of God.

Walking in our faith encourages us to draw closer to God, but it's also a witness to those around us. Never underestimate a prayer, a phone call, a word of encouragement, a text message, or what you share about what God is doing in your life. God uses all things to show all people that He is God. He desires to be in a relationship with all people, because we're all made in the image of God.

After seeing Jesus calm the storm, the disciples believed that He was the Messiah. Rahab could see that the God of Israel was mighty, powerful, and the true and living God. If God worked this way in the Bible, then I believe that He also works in our situations to witness to us and others that He is God!

Fifteen

GOD IS FAITHFUL

I WISH I could tell you that no one I've cared about has ever disappointed, betrayed, or angered me, but unfortunately, I can't say that. I can't even say that about myself. I know that I have unintentionally hurt others with my words and actions. These are memories I wish I could erase. Why do we hurt each other? Because we're not perfect. We live in a sinful world, and unless we get our relationship with God right through Jesus, we will keep hurting people. That's the power of the gospel—we can be saved from our sin and live a good and holy life through the Holy Spirit. But what is also amazing is that there is one person who is consistent, good, and faithful to all of us, and that person is God!

Growing up, I often heard people in church say things like, "God has not failed me" or "God is good." That made sense to me as long as life was good. But as I got older, I didn't understand those sayings, because I went through very hard and traumatic situations. I asked myself the question, "Why do people say God is good when this happened to me?" I'm sure you've had the same questions or feelings. Some things in life just don't make sense. But through time, prayer, and reflection, I can now understand

and say with others that despite everything that has happened to me, God is good and faithful.

We can testify that God is good and faithful because of the stories recorded in our Bible. If you take the time to survey the Bible from beginning to end, you'll read about our faithful God.

Right from the beginning, in the book of Genesis, we see a faithful God. When God created Adam and Eve, He saw that what He'd made was good, but because of their disobedience to Him, sin entered the world. But even then, God covered them and showed them grace. God was faithful.

Generations after Adam and Eve, God made a covenant with His servant Abraham. God promised Abraham a son, and that his descendants would be as numerous as the stars. Everything God promised to Abraham came true. Abraham had his promised son, Isaac. God kept His word and was faithful to Abraham.

God's faithfulness continued through Abraham's son Isaac. Isaac had his son Jacob, and through his two wives and two servants, he had twelve sons altogether. Even though Jacob was deceitful and manipulative, that didn't change God's plan. God didn't disown Jacob; rather, He worked out His plan and promises through Jacob and his children. God was faithful to Jacob despite his shortcomings.

Then through one of Jacob's sons, Joseph, God worked out His plan for the Jewish people. Even though Joseph was betrayed by his brothers and suffered greatly, God used him to bless his family and spare His people. God was faithful to Joseph and His people.

After the death of Joseph, his brothers, and their children, their descendants began to multiply, and Egypt began to fear the people. The Egyptians were concerned about the Jews overpowering them, so they made them slaves for over four hundred years. Just think about the length of this oppression and the sadness of God's people. In their bondage, the people of God cried out to Him, and He heard their cry. God sent Moses to lead them out of Egypt to the promised land. God was faithful and saved His people.

When the people of God went into the promised land, Joshua became their new leader. When it was time, the people conquered the land promised by God, but unfortunately, they broke their faithfulness to God. But even then, God was still faithful to His people. He sent them leaders like Gideon, Samson, and Deborah (these were judges) to help the people stay on track. But even in God's grace and mercy, the people continuously sinned and were punished for it. Yet every time God would bail them out. God was faithful to His people despite their lack of faithfulness to Him.

Eventually, the people of God asked for a king. At the time, the people chose Saul to be their earthly king. But King Saul wasn't faithful to God; he was disobedient. This is why the prophet Samuel anointed David to be the next king.

David was Israel's greatest king, because he was a man after God's heart. But David still fell short of the kind of king God had in mind for His people and the world. For God wanted a perfect, eternal, and ultimate king for His people, but the time wasn't right for that king to be revealed. So while God was waiting for the right time, He allowed His people to have human kings, like David and others kings, to lead them. God continued to be faithful.

After King David died, Solomon, his son, became king. Unfortunately, Solomon was unfaithful to God, and he married many foreign women and worshipped their pagan gods. This began the downfall of God's people. Despite the people's unfaithfulness to God, He sent great prophets like Elijah, Elisha, Isaiah, and Jeremiah to lead the people back in the right direction. But the people kept on sinning over and over again.

God warned His people to repent, but then the inevitable happened. The beautiful temple of God, built under King Solomon's leadership, was destroyed, and Israel was overtaken by the Babylonians and taken into captivity. Everything was ruined. They were now slaves to the Babylonians. Life was hard, but God didn't remain merciless. He sent the prophets Daniel and Ezekiel and others to preach a message of hope—that they would be delivered out of their trouble and that the Messiah would come.

After God's people came out of exile, they began to rebuild their homes and their synagogue. Many had to return to Jerusalem. This was a journey, and even then, God still loved His people. God was faithful and sent people like Ezra and Nehemiah to minister to His people.

You would think that after all the times God had to intervene and save His people from their disobedience and sin, that He'd eventually stop showing grace and mercy. Perhaps we would say that God's supply of grace came to an end. But think again. God had something amazing planned. He was preparing the world for His greatest gift. During four hundred years of silence, something strong was brewing. That something was the coming king—Jesus.

Jesus entered the world humbly through a virgin named Mary. He could have come into the world with His sword and His power, but He chose to come quietly. After entering the world, Jesus grew in wisdom, favour, and stature. He taught the gospel, preached the Word, and healed the sick. He was the image of the invisible God. God's Son. The Messiah. God in the flesh. He was fully God and fully man.

This was the promised Son talked about in the Old Testament. He was the suffering servant and the shoot of Jesse, as preached by Isaiah. He was the prophesied man riding on the donkey, spoken of by the prophet Zechariah. He was the man who would be born in Bethlehem, as prophesied by the prophet Micah.

Why did God keep holding on to His people? Why didn't God just throw His hands up in the air and wipe out humanity? Why not put an end to this tormenting, inconsistent relationship? Clearly, according to the stories in the Bible, we're incapable of being faithful to God.

God didn't give up on us because God is faithful. His faithfulness to us isn't dependent on our faithfulness to Him. Even though we don't deserve it, and we certainly haven't held up our end of the bargain, God doesn't leave us. Instead, He sent Jesus to save us from our sins, because we couldn't help ourselves. Without Jesus, we'd be drowning in spiritual debt, but because of His death and resurrection, the price for our sins has been paid, and we no longer have to live in darkness. A Light has entered into the world, and we receive this Light by accepting Jesus as our Lord and Saviour. This is wonderful news! News that we can't comprehend but that has the power to transform our lives.

When I think about how much God loves us and what He was willing to do to save us, it gets me every time. My mind can't comprehend that kind of faithfulness. But this is who God is—He is faithful. Faithful in the past, faithful in the present, and faithful in the future. We might think that our story ends here, but it doesn't. One day Jesus will return to the earth—not as a baby, but as a king. He will be on a horse and will be glorified, and He will be called Faithful and True (Revelation 19:11). There will be a new earth and a new heaven, and those who have accepted Him as Lord and Saviour will live! What wonderful news! He truly is the King of kings and Lord of lords.

When God could have stopped giving His time, love, and mercy to us, He didn't. He kept giving, giving, and giving. I don't think there will ever be another person in this world who loves us the way our God loves us. He willingly laid down His life for us so that we would have life. His grace is endless, and His love is deep. This is our God—faithful. Faithful to His people and faithful to the end. All that's left for us to decide is if we want to follow this God. The choice is ours. Will we have faith in God and trust Him?